Achieving
Personal
Well-Being

Achieving

Personal Well-Being

How to discover and balance your physical and emotional needs

JAMES CHALMERS
2nd edition

How To Books

Published by How To Books Ltd, 3 Newtec Place,
Magdalen Road, Oxford OX4 1RE. United Kingdom.
Tel: (01865) 793806. Fax: (01865) 248780.
email: info@howtobooks.co.uk
www.howtobooks.co.uk

British Library Cataloguing in Publication Data
A catalogue record for this book is available from
the British Library

Cover design by Shireen Nathoo Design
Cover image PhotoDisc
Cartoons by Mike Flanagan

Produced for How To Books by Deer Park Productions
Typeset by PDQ Typesetting, Stoke-on-Trent, Staffs.
Printed and bound by Cromwell Press, Trowbridge, Wiltshire

NOTE: The material contained in this book is set out in good
faith for general guidance and no liability can be accepted
for loss or expense incurred as a result of relying in particular
circumstances on statements made in the book. The laws and
regulations are complex and liable to change, and readers should
check the current position with the relevant authorities before
making personal arrangements.

Contents

List of illustrations   7

Preface   9

1 Finding your balance point   11
   Understanding yourself   11
   Keeping the enemy at bay   13
   Living on earth   14
   Finding out about yourself   17
   Checklist of key points   21
   Case studies   22

2 Following the sun   24
   Marking out the sky   24
   Finding your birth sign   28
   Changing the meaning of the signs   35
   Checklist of key points   36
   Case studies   37

3 Finding your body and mind type   38
   Determining your profile   38
   Investigating personality   38
   Identifying your bio-type   52
   Writing up your personal profile   56
   Checklist of key points   58
   Case studies   58

4 Living with daylight   60
   Soaking up the sun   60
   Receiving the right signals   64
   Counting the daylight hours   68
   Working with artificial light   72
   Taking the right dose of daylight   76
   Checklist of key points   78
   Case studies   80

5   Achieving a balance   **82**
    Reviewing the situation   82
    Counting calories   83
    Fending off excesses   90
    Cutting out excesses   91
    Eliminating deficiencies   101
    Taking personal action   107
    Checklist of key points   111
    Case studies   112

6   Building in well-being   **114**
    Influencing our senses   114
    Unlocking the influences   117
    Providing the answers   119
    Checklist of key points   130
    Case studies   132

Glossary   134

Further Reading   138

Useful Addresses   140

Index   141

List of Illustrations

1. Representing your balance point   12
2. The unbalance and recovery cycle   14
3. The left and right side of your brain   20
4. The path of the sun inside the celestial sphere   26
5. The zodiac, or astrological calendar   29
6. Zodiac location chart for the northern hemisphere   32
7. Zodiac location chart for the southern hemisphere   33
8. The Aries scorecard   40
9. The Taurus scorecard   41
10. The Gemini scorecard   42
11. The Cancer scorecard   43
12. The Leo scorecard   44
13. The Virgo scorecard   45
14. The Libra scorecard   46
15. The Scorpio scorecard   47
16. The Sagittarius scorecard   48
17. The Capricorn scorecard   49
18. The Aquarius scorecard   50
19. The Pisces scorecard   51
20. The bio-type scorecard   54
21. Example of completed personal profile card   57
22. Sunlight and vitamin D levels   63
23. The electromagnetic spectrum   65
24. The hypothalamus, pituitary and pineal   68
25. Daylight guidelines   77
26. Foods that suit the two bio-types   89
27. Summary table of toxins   100
28. The vitamin table   105
29. The mineral table   106
30. Example of a completed personal action plan   109
31. The case study cottage – front view   121
32. The case study cottage – plans   122

Preface
to the second edition

The starting point for my investigations into well-being was a wide range of questions about the body and mind. Why can some people eat what they like without putting on weight? Can personality be reliably linked to the zodiac signs? Is there such a thing as sick building syndrome? When people say they feel depressed because of a lack of sunshine, is this a physical or emotional reaction?

I discovered that all these questions had already been answered. But the information was spread across a variety of publications. And each piece of information represented only part of a much larger picture. To achieve well-being, we need to deal with *all* our physical and emotional needs, not just one or two in isolation. Bringing all the various ideas together, was the task I set myself when I started to write this book.

The second edition has allowed me to add further important information, resulting from my continuing research. It has also become more apparent how even the smallest of changes to our diet, living and working conditions, and levels of natural daylight, can have a major impact on our health and welfare. So it's worth stressing that achieving personal well-being is all about making a number of small adjustments to your diet and lifestyle, each one of which on its own may not appear to be of much significance.

As you work your way through the book, you will build up a picture of yourself. Much of this information will be recorded on the scorecards provided, but you may also like to jot down notes, with page references, in case you want to go back over any of the points.

You may find that some of the advice appears to contradict popular opinion. But I expect you have already tried all the usual things without much success. So perhaps now is time for a different approach.

So good luck with your journey to well-being and I trust you will find this book both interesting and helpful.

James Chalmers

1

Finding Your Balance Point

UNDERSTANDING YOURSELF

Your body and mind are inextricably linked. So there is a lot of truth in the saying:

> Healthy body, healthy mind.

The reverse:

> Healthy mind, healthy body

is also true.

Managing well-being

There are plenty of books and videos available offering advice on all aspects of physical and emotional well-being. These, however, tend to specialise in individual subject areas, for example: aerobic exercises, improving relationships and so on.

Attending to physical or emotional needs in isolation will not necessarily result in an improvement in your overall well-being. This book deals with achieving well-being by managing the combined needs of your body and mind.

Defining your balance point

Your body and mind balance point is represented by the set of scales, illustrated in Figure 1.

The figures on each side are:

Left	Right
Your physical and emotional needs	What your environment has to offer

Physical and emotional well-being is all about achieving and maintaining a balance.

> **You must match your needs to what your environment has to offer.**

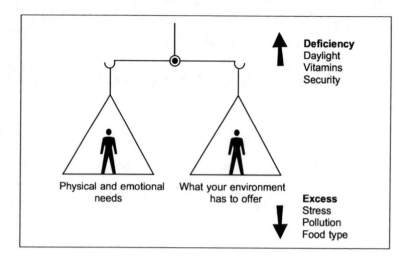

Fig. 1. Representing your balance point.

Getting out of balance

You will get out of balance as a result of:

1. *A deficiency*: you are deprived of something that is essential to your needs.

2. *An excess*: you receive something that you don't need, or, you receive something you normally require, but in excessive amounts.

   Figure 1 indicates some examples of common deficiencies and excesses.

   Getting out of balance can have a direct and serious effect on your well-being. For example, you may:

- develop an illness
- put on weight
- become unhappy at work
- experience difficulties with a relationship
- become uncertain about your role in life.

Taking steps to well-being

The key points about the effects of balance and your physical and emotional well-being are:

1. Significant problems can be caused by even an insignificant excess or deficiency.

2. Physical and emotional problems are closely linked – very often one will lead to the other.

3. It is usually difficult to identify the root cause of a decline in well-being.

   The key steps to well-being are:

1. Understand the things that influence you.

2. Find out what sort of person you are.

3. Work out your individual needs.

4. Take action to adjust your needs.

KEEPING THE ENEMY AT BAY

The point at which you begin to notice something is wrong does not necessarily mark the point at which a person gets out of balance. The human body is very resilient to excesses and deficiencies. It may be years before the effects of any unbalance are noticed.

Noticing something is wrong

Most people will be able to come up with an example of someone they know who lived an apparently healthy life until the age of 99, in spite of smoking 20 cigarettes a day and getting through a bottle of scotch a week. Such stories, however, merely demonstrate the varying degree to which people can cope with excessive abuse of their bodies.

Recovering your balance

Fortunately the human body and mind are able to repair much of the damage that results from excesses or deficiencies.

   Important key points for recovering your balance are:

1. Take action as soon as you know that you are in an unbalanced situation. Ideally this should be before you are aware of anything going wrong.

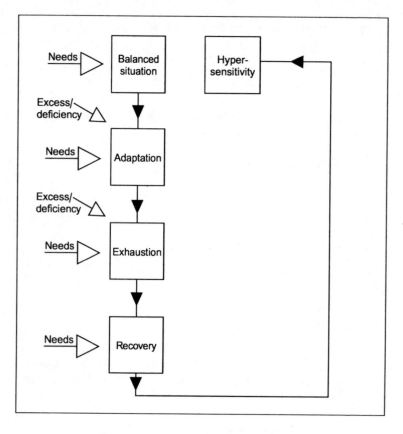

Fig. 2. The unbalance and recovery cycle.

2. Don't fall back into your old habits after recovery – your resistance will not be as strong the second time around.

The unbalance and recovery cycle is illustrated in Figure 2. You will be aware of a problem in the **exhaustion** stage. This is when your mind or body gives up the fight. After recovery you are in the **hypersensitive** stage. If you then resume the excess or deficiency, the problems will be much worse than before.

LIVING ON EARTH

Half of all the air required to sustain human life on earth is contained within a band just four miles high. This is relatively small compared with the size of the earth, which is about 8000 miles in diameter.

Understanding how the environment influences our lives
There are two influences that control our lives.

1. **Terrestrial**: forces that originate at or on the surface of the earth. Examples include air temperature, food and music.

2. **Astral**: forces that originate beyond the earth's atmosphere. Examples include solar radiation, moonlight and the cycle of night and day.

Both the terrestrial and astral influences can be further subdivided into:

- *physical*: influences that affect people by a measurable force or energy

- *sensory*: influences that are received by our senses and which cannot in most cases be measured.

Exercise one
Pick out a landmark you know to be four miles away, for example on the other side of a valley. Use this to gauge the height of the life-sustaining air above your head. This will give you a feel for how thin and precious our atmosphere is.

Exercise two
List the influences you think play a part in our lives. Place them under the main headings of terrestrial and astral. Then mark which ones are physical and which are sensory.

Measuring time
Our ancestors had no clocks or printed calendars. They divided the year into months and seasons by observing the position of the sun against the background of stars.

The stars are grouped into constellations. Our ancestors saw the constellations as the shapes and outlines of mythical people and animals. There are around 80 named constellations and they form a giant map across the night sky. Most still carry the names given to them thousands of years ago.

The sun always moves in front of the same twelve constellations.

These twelve constellations are called the zodiac. This gave people a method of dividing up the year into twelve equal divisions – the astrological calendar.

We will be referring to the astrological calendar quite a lot in this book, because it is a useful method of plotting the position of the sun and indicating levels of solar radiation, which is the most important astral influence.

Labelling your birthday

The majority of animals produce young only at a certain time of the year, but human children can be born at any time of the year. We have continued the tradition of associating a birth date with a zodiac constellation. For example, a baby born on 30 January falls within the zodiac sign of Aquarius.

Many people also like to believe that each zodiac sign carries with it a distinct personality. If we accept this as a reasonable assumption, then we can use the standard zodiac personality profiles as an indicator of individual emotional needs.

An explanation of why personality profiles vary because of date of birth is given in Chapter 4. However, the zodiac signs are only used here as a source of personality profiles. This book does not discuss horoscopes and prediction.

Outlining the development of astronomy

Astronomy developed from astrology, after the telescope was invented. Astronomy is much more about accurate measurement, whereas astrology was based mainly on observation.

Astronomers still use the astrology star map to identify areas in the night sky. So astrology should not be dismissed entirely as irrelevant ancient history.

The Seven Stars

Before the invention of the telescope, there were only five planets visible: Mercury, Venus, Mars, Jupiter and Saturn. Like the sun, these also move in relation to the fixed background of the star map.

The visible five planets, together with the sun and the moon, are traditionally known as *The Seven Stars*. Many English public houses are called *The Seven Stars*, but usually the name is wrongly attributed to the constellation of the plough.

FINDING OUT ABOUT YOURSELF

The standard astrology personality profiles give us a method of identifying individual emotional needs. To help us sort out physical requirements, we need to be clear how our nervous systems work.

Sending messages

You are like a city with its own underground railway. The functioning of the city depends not only on the transmission of messages between offices by telephone, fax and e-mail, but also on an army of messengers who carry information by hand. They travel on the underground, getting on and off at the stations to receive and deliver instructions to the right buildings.

Understanding the nervous system

1. The *central nervous system* works by electric impulses supplied to the muscles through the spinal cord. This is the equivalent of the telephone, faxes and e-mails in our imaginary city.

2. The *endocrine nervous system* works by glands releasing hormones into the bloodstream, which are then picked up by glands further round the body. This is the equivalent of the messengers travelling by the underground railway.

Designing your body

What type of person you are depends very much on the nature of your **endocrine nervous system**. It's the blue-print of what you are.

Keypoints

1. Your endocrine nervous system is in control of many of your body functions, for example:
   - the digestion of food
   - your growth from childhood into a mature adult
   - your sex drive
   - the menstrual cycle
   - the way you think.

2. Your endocrine nervous system operates almost entirely subconsciously so that you are not aware of what it is doing, and you can't consciously intervene.
   - It links to the central nervous system for some things, *eg* adrenalin production to get you out of danger fast.

- It has essential needs for effective operation, *eg* trace elements in your food.
- It will stand quite a bit of abuse for a while, before it starts to go wrong and protest.
- It has some links to the outside world, *eg* it tells you to go to sleep when it gets dark.

Typing biochemically

In America, in the late 1970s, a Dr Kelley developed the idea of **metabolic typing**. This means classifying people according to how their nervous system works. It was done by observation, rather than strict scientific measurement. The approach was very like how our ancestors built up a view of our place in the universe using astrology.

Metabolic typing is also known as **biochemical typing**. In this book it has been shortened to **bio-typing**. Bio-typing is a very useful tool for helping us judge how our bodies work.

Thinking left or right

Our brain has two halves – the left and the right. Each half has its own area of responsibility when it comes to thinking.

The right side is like the marketing department of a business. It is responsible for coming up with good ideas for increasing company sales.

The left side is like the accounts department. This department needs to keep a tight control over the wild ideas from marketing. The left side tends to dominate the right side.

The brain's thinking responsibilities can be summarised as follows:

Left side	*Right side*
Analytical and verbal	Intuitive and spatial
Good for maths and anything digital by nature.	Good for creative work and anything analogue in nature.

Note
This has nothing to do with being right or left handed. The right side of the brain always does the same thing in all people.

Freeing up our minds

Most of the time the left side of our brain overrules the right side. This tends to stifle creative thinking. Artists, however, have the ability to get the right side of their brains to ignore what the left side is saying.

Some situations can free up the right side and lead to that sudden and unexpected flash of inspiration – that good idea that solves a difficult problem. So it is useful to know when this is most likely to occur.

The following situations are typical:

1. Just as you are about to fall asleep.

2. During the short period when you wake during the night as a result of an unexpected noise or other disturbance.

3. Whilst swimming.

4. Driving a car on an open road with very little traffic about.

People who are employed in creative work, such as writers and designers, should always have a notebook or a cassette recorder to hand, wherever they are. A flash of inspiration can soon be forgotten as the more logical left brain talks you out of it. So write it down or record it immediately, before that good idea is lost for ever.

Controlling our bodies

What we have just been looking at has been related to thinking, which is something we do consciously. What we are not conscious of is our brain controlling our body functions. For example, we do not have to think about what we are eating so that our body delivers the correct fluids to digest the food. This happens automatically.

The endocrine nervous system is also known as the **autonomic nervous system**. Autonomic is another way of saying automatic.

The way in which the endocrine nervous system links to the brain is illustrated in Figure 3. The pituitary gland is at the top of your neck, just under your brain.

The pituitary has two parts. One is linked to the left side of the brain and the other to the right side of the brain.

Dividing responsibilities

If you follow the lines through on the diagram illustrated in Figure 3, you will see that:

● *The right side of your brain* has responsibility for looking after the digestion of food and the immune system, which fights off infections. Technically this is known as the **parasympathetic nervous system**.

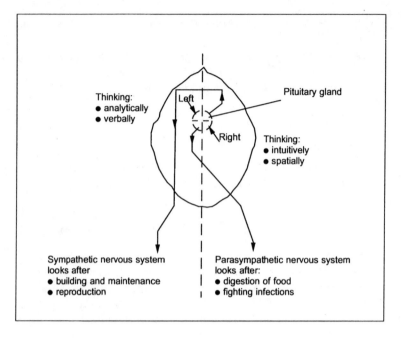

Fig. 3. The left and right side of your brain.

- *The left side of your brain* has responsibility for keeping your bones and tissues in good order by extracting the necessary material from the food you eat. It also produces the male and female hormones essential for human reproduction. Technically this is known as the **sympathetic nervous system**.

Defining your bio-type
Bio-typing classifies people according to the dominance of the left or right side of the brain. The technical terms are: **sympathetic dominant** or **parasympathetic dominant**. But we shall use the simpler terms: left biased or right biased.

You can determine what sort of nervous system you have by observing key characteristics, such as sleep patterns. A score card to do this is available in Chapter 3.

Note
Don't jump to any hasty conclusions about yourself. For example, if you are artistic, this does not necessarily mean you have a right biased nervous system.

CHECKLIST OF KEY POINTS

Understanding yourself
1. Your body and mind are inextricably linked.

2. Physical and emotional needs must be managed together.

3. Well-being is balancing your needs with what the environment has to offer.

4. You can get out of balance as a result of either a deficiency or an excess.

5. This book shows you how to achieve well-being by getting your body and mind into balance.

Getting out of balance
1. Your mind and body will resist excesses and deficiencies for as long as it can.

2. When either the mind or body can no longer resist, you will know that something is wrong and you may become ill.

3. If the excess or deficiency is corrected, you can recover, but you will then be hypersensitive to whatever it was that caused the problem.

Your environment
1. Our lives are controlled by terrestrial and astral influences.

2. These influences can be either physical or sensory.

3. The position of the sun is the basis of the astrological calendar.

4. Personality can be linked to date of birth.

Finding out about yourself
1. The type of person you are depends on the nature of the endocrine nervous system.

2. The endocrine nervous system is autonomic.

3. Your brain has a left and right side. The right side is creative.

The left side is analytical.

4. The left and right side of the brain also controls body functions through the endocrine nervous system.

5. Your bio-type can be defined as either left or right biased.

CASE STUDIES

Martin spots tunes at any time of the day
Martin is the regional sales manager for a national chain of computer software stores. In his spare time he is the singer–songwriter in a rock band.

Martin composes his songs while sitting at his piano. But he relies on inspiration coming to him at all sorts of unexpected moments. For example lying in the bath, driving between the computer stores and during boring sales meetings.

So that he never misses any of these exciting ideas, Martin always has a notebook to hand and a small cassette recorder in his pocket.

Alison's sunshine theory is in the right direction
Alison is a 40-year-old mother of two, who works full time in the orders department of a large communications company. She works with 20 other people in an office, each sitting at a personal computer. Their job is to input order details, received by phone and letter.

Alison is feeling increasingly depressed. She dislikes her job because it is undemanding and monotonous. She also finds it difficult to get on with the other people. More worrying is that there are signs that she may be developing arthritis.

Alison's doctor gives her some tablets to help ease the pains in her joints. He tells her that it is a sign of age, and she will just have to live with it.

Alison is yearning to have a holiday in Spain. As a teenager, she spent every summer on the Costa del Sol, but she hasn't been back there for a number of years. She has noticed that even a short break of a few days in her garden seems to help with her arthritis. As a result she is less depressed.

Alison's body and mind are out of balance. To return to well-being, she needs to identify the excesses or deficiencies that are causing the problem.

Stone walls free Mike's mind

Mike has been an interior designer for 20 years. Examples of his work can be found all over Europe, in houses, hotels and offices. Lately his ideas appear to have gone stale, and the level of enquiries from potential clients is significantly lower than it was a year ago.

Recently Mike has invested in modern technology, in the hope that this would help, but on the contrary it only makes the situation worse.

Mike takes a weekend break in a cottage in Yorkshire. He notices that all the surrounding fields are enclosed by dry stone walls. These walls, he realises, could only have been built through intuition, as each stone is a different size and shape.

This realisation has great influence on him and when he returns home, he starts to treat his computer more as a tool, than as something that thinks. He begins to design intuitively again, and his designs take on a new freshness. Very soon his business is back on its feet.

2

Following the Sun

MARKING OUT THE SKY

These days we don't need to be able to work out what time of year it is from the position of the stars. But understanding how the astrological calendar works will allow you to:

- Observe the level of daylight changes over the year. This is very helpful for our discussions in Chapter 4, about the links between daylight and well-being.

- Discover how your birth date ties in with your zodiac sign. This will give you confidence in the concept of linking personality to birth date.

- Find your own zodiac sign in the night sky. This is a stimulating experience, bringing you into contact with the vast scale of the heavens.

Choosing a viewpoint

To view the night sky you will need to choose a suitable vantage point. The best place will have the following features:

1. It will be on higher ground than its surroundings.

2. It should have a clear view to the south, if you live in Europe, the USA or Asia, *ie* the northern hemisphere. But if you live in South Africa, Australia or New Zealand – the southern hemisphere – you will need a clear view to the north.

3. It should have an unobstructed view towards the horizon, without any tall trees, buildings or high hills getting in the way.

4. It should be away from street lighting and the light from buildings.

5. It should also be a place that you can easily find to return to, both during the day and the night, and at any time of the year.

Aligning your viewpoint

When you want to find the zodiac signs in the night sky, you will need to know where:

- south is – in the northern hemisphere, and
- north is – in the southern hemisphere.

Here are the key steps to finding and marking either south or north. You will use this to help you find your birth sign.

1. Visit your viewpoint during the day.

2. Either (a) use a magnetic compass to find the correct direction – magnetic north and south is near enough – don't worry about having to make a correction to get true north or south. Or (b) note the direction of the sun at midday – this means true midday, *ie* GMT in the UK – so you may have to allow for summer daylight saving hours at some times in the year.

3. Pick a landmark that lies due south, or north for the southern hemisphere. This will need to be visible in the dark. Examples of markers are: a small copse, a farmhouse or a low hill in the distance.

Gazing at heaven

When you stand at your viewpoint at night, the stars appear to be fixed to the inside of a giant inverted pudding bowl. This bowl is known as the **celestial sphere**.

If you were to stand there for long enough, you would notice that the whole of the celestial sphere is moving slowly from east to west. This is because the earth is turning.

Our ancestors had no way of knowing that the stars are all at different distances from the earth, and we still find it easier to map the stars as if they are on the inside of a huge globe enveloping the earth.

Planetariums give illustrated shows about astronomy to an audience sitting inside a huge dome. The images of the stars are projected onto the inside of the dome above the audience's heads, thus re-creating the celestial sphere.

Thinking about the sun

Return to your viewpoint during the day, after you've looked at the night sky. During daylight hours the celestial sphere is still there, but you can't see the stars because the sun is so bright.

Now think about the path of the sun across the sky:

- In the summer it crosses from east to west, tracing out a curve high in the sky.

- In winter the path is still a curve, but much lower down.

- The path of the sun is on the inside of the celestial sphere, as illustrated by Figure 4.

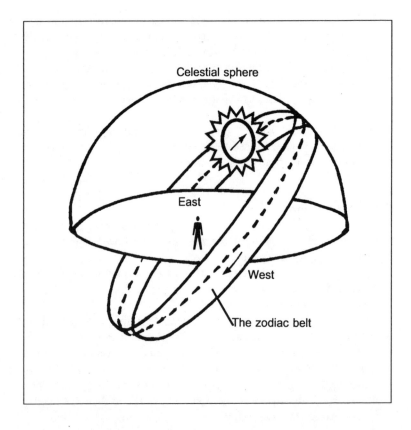

Fig. 4. The path of the sun inside the celestial sphere.

Exercise

When you are at your viewpoint during daylight, think very hard about the sun being inside the celestial sphere. Close your eyes for a while, and imagine the star-studded dome over your head and the sun moving just in front of it. But please be careful not to stare at the sun directly, as it can damage your eyes.

Tracing out a path

The sun always follows the same path against the background of star constellations – for summer and winter and for the northern or southern hemisphere.

Think of the sun as a car being driven down the middle of a road, following the broken centre line, with the road edges some distance away on either side. This imaginary road around the celestial sphere is called the **zodiac belt**. There are twelve star constellations around the belt, and these are the twelve signs of the zodiac. The zodiac constellations lie directly behind the path of the sun, between the imaginary road edges.

The zodiac signs can't be seen during the day, but the zodiac belt extends right around the earth, so the other half is visible at night.

The arrows in Figure 4 indicate the movement of both the sun and the zodiac belt. This can be summed up as follows.

- The zodiac belt moves from east to west.

- The sun also moves from east to west.

- The sun takes 24 hours to go round the earth.

- The zodiac belt takes less than 24 hours to move right round the earth.

- Because the zodiac belt is moving a little faster than the sun, the sun gradually moves backwards against the background of the zodiac belt.

- The sun moves through all twelve zodiac constellations, to arrive back where it started, over a period of a year.

Dividing up the year

The movement of the sun in relation to the zodiac constellations lying behind it provided an effective method of dividing up the year into twelve equal parts. So the zodiac's primary role was as a calendar.

The zodiac calendar is illustrated in Figure 5. The key points are:

1. The twelve pictures of the zodiac signs show how they look in the night sky.

2. The dates indicate when the sun is within each zodiac sign.

3. Aries is traditionally the first sign as it marked the beginning of the northern hemisphere spring.

4. The pictures of the zodiac constellations for star gazers in the southern hemisphere need to be turned upside down to match how they look in the sky.

Understanding the inadequacies of the zodiac calendar

The zodiac, or astrological calendar, illustrated in Figure 5, looks similar to our modern calendar, which is also divided up into twelve roughly equal periods.

But the zodiac calendar does have its problems.

1. Because the sun is in front of the zodiac sign when it is marking that period of the year, the sun blots out the stars so you can't see it.

2. Astrologers had to be employed to say what time of the year it was. They were the only people able to work out the position of the sun in relation to the zodiac signs. This made astrologers powerful and rich.

In the next section of this chapter, we will see how to find your own zodiac sign in the night sky, without needing the skills of an astrologer.

FINDING YOUR BIRTH SIGN

Finding your own birth sign in the night sky is an interesting and stimulating experience.

Experiencing astrology

Being in visual contact with your own birth sign is experiencing astrology first hand. You will find this much more informative and

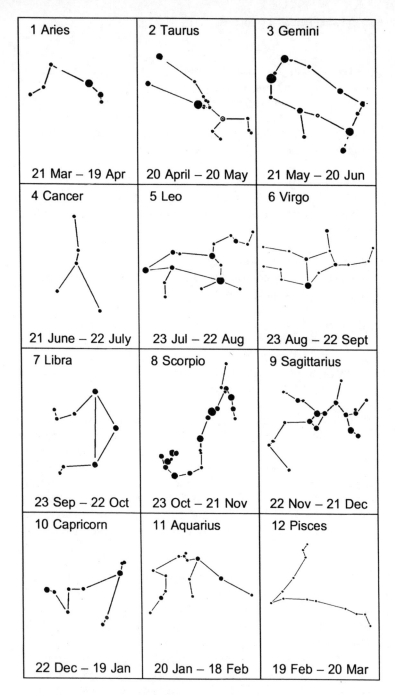

1 Aries	2 Taurus	3 Gemini
21 Mar – 19 Apr	20 April – 20 May	21 May – 20 Jun
4 Cancer	5 Leo	6 Virgo
21 June – 22 July	23 Jul – 22 Aug	23 Aug – 22 Sept
7 Libra	8 Scorpio	9 Sagittarius
23 Sep – 22 Oct	23 Oct – 21 Nov	22 Nov – 21 Dec
10 Capricorn	11 Aquarius	12 Pisces
22 Dec – 19 Jan	20 Jan – 18 Feb	19 Feb – 20 Mar

Fig. 5. The zodiac, or astrological calendar.

pleasurable than just reading about your own star-sign traits in a book or newspaper horoscope.

Gazing up at your zodiac constellation means being able to say:

> 'That's my birth sign. When I was born the sun was lying within that constellation.'

Overcoming problems

There are, however, some problems that need to be overcome when looking for your birth sign. The following list outlines each problem and provides a solution.

1. At the time of your birthday, the sun blots out your birth sign, because it's in front of it. *Solution*: Look for your birth sign at a time other than near to your birthday.

2. It's not worth wasting a lot of time outside, unless the sky is reasonably cloudless. You need to be able to see quite large areas of the sky, and clouds will block your view. *Solution*: Be ready, by knowing exactly what you are going out to look for. Then wait patiently until the right opportunity arises.

3. Britain is not the best place to see all of the zodiac signs, because it's too far north of the equator. Some of the signs are very near the horizon in the summer months, and these can easily be hidden by trees and hills. *Solution*: A high vantage point will help, and even better is a clear view to the south across the open sea. If you're going on holiday to France or Spain, make sure you take this book with you. Both these countries have the advantage of a more southerly latitude and they also tend to have clearer skies.

4. Astronomy books have illustrations of the night sky, with all the constellations labelled, including the zodiac signs. These star maps usually include a dotted line, to show the path the sun follows through the zodiac belt. This dotted line is called the **ecliptic**.

    In the summer months, when the path of the sun is high in the sky, you might also expect the ecliptic to be high in the sky during the hours of darkness. But the opposite is true. At night, in the summer, the zodiac belt is down near the horizon. So it's easy to get confused and look in the wrong place for the zodiac constellations. *Solution*: This book gives a simple and straight-forward method of how to find the zodiac signs, by telling you *when* and *where* to look in the night sky.

Charting the zodiac signs

Two charts are provided to help you to locate all the zodiac signs. The first chart is for people in the northern hemisphere, the second is for people in the southern hemisphere. Details of the two charts are summarised below.

Chart	Northern	Southern
Illustrated in	Figure 6	Figure 7
Correct for a latitude of	50° north	40° south
Typical location	London UK	Wellington, New Zealand
Time of month	15th day	15th day
Time of viewing	10p.m.	10p.m.

Notes
1. For places nearer the equator, the signs will be higher in the sky than indicated on the charts.

2. The charts are correct for the middle of the month – around the fifteenth day. However, use of the charts is fairly flexible, and you can make corrections if you are star gazing at some other time. This is explained later.

3. 10p.m. means actual time, not a time adjusted for daylight saving. During the summer months in the UK, 11p.m. is the equivalent time. But in practice, the one hour will make very little difference to the position of the signs.

Explaining how the charts work

Before we look at the steps to take to find the zodiac signs in the night sky, let's have a quick look at the charts to clarify some of the details. Refer either to Figure 6 or Figure 7, depending on where you live.

The quarter circles down the left-hand side represent the celestial sphere:

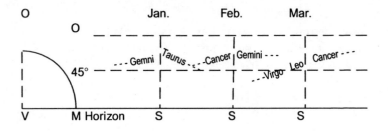

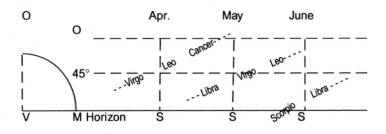

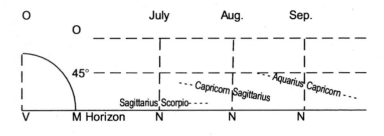

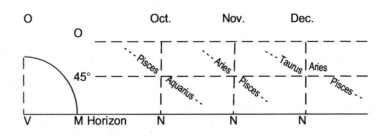

Fig. 6. Zodiac location chart for the northern hemisphere.

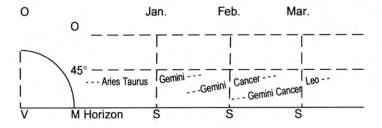

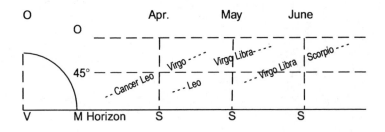

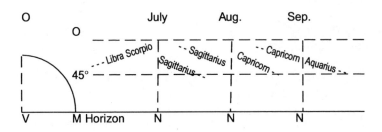

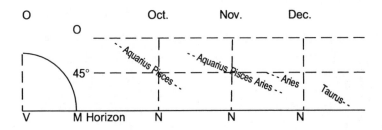

Fig. 7. Zodiac location chart for the southern hemisphere.

- **V** is where you are standing at your viewpoint.

- **M** is the landmark that gives you the direction of south (north in the southern hemisphere)

- **O** is the point directly over your head.

To the right of each of the quarter circles are a series of views to the south (or north for the southern hemisphere). The overhead point is marked by the upper dotted line. Half-way between the horizon and the overhead point is another dotted line. This is at a 45 degree angle from where you are standing.

Locating 45 degrees
Hold this book at arm's length, closed and vertical. Keeping your arm straight, you will be able to fill in from the horizon to the overhead point with the height of four books. The 45 degree point is two books up from the horizon.

Another useful tip is that the size of the zodiac constellations are about the same size as the book held at arm's length and horizontal.

Using the chart
The key steps for using the zodiac location chart are as follows:

1. Stand at your viewpoint at approximately 10p.m. facing south (or north for the southern hemisphere).

2. Select the correct month and read which signs are next to the vertical line.

3. Check what the signs will look like from the illustrations in Figure 5. (Turn the book upside down for the southern hemisphere.)

4. From the chart, estimate the position of the sign in the sky – in relation to:
   – the horizon
   – the overhead point
   – the 45 degree point
   – your landmark, which is the vertical dotted line on the chart under the month name.

5. Look at the sky to see the sign in the expected position.

Examples
1. In the northern hemisphere, Gemini can be seen in January, to the left of the south landmark, just above the 45 degree point. Taurus will be seen to the right of Gemini.

2. In April in the southern hemisphere Leo is to the left of the north landmark, below the 45 degree point. Virgo is to the right of the north landmark, above the 45 degree point.

CHANGING THE MEANING OF THE SIGNS

Over time the appearance of the star map has been gradually changing. However, because astrology is based on trends rather than on accurate measurements, these changes need not worry us unduly.

Moving the tropics

The sun at its most northerly point is above **the tropic of Cancer**. This is on 21 June, at the summer solstice. This date used to be well inside the zodiac constellation of Cancer, which gave the tropic its name. But the date has now moved up to Gemini. So you may find different dates given for the zodiac signs in different publications.

If your birth date is very close to an adjacent sign, you may be unsure of exactly where you belong. We will deal with this possible point of confusion in the next chapter, when we look at the personality profiles of each birth sign.

Heralding a new age

The beginning of the northern hemisphere spring is marked by the sun moving north of the equator. In the early days of astrology, this date was in Aries. This is why Aries is traditionally the first sign of the zodiac. But 2000 years ago the first day of spring moved into Pisces.

Pisces represents two fish joined at their tails. The fish is a Christian symbol, which ties in with the birth of Christ at the beginning of the age of Pisces.

The next zodiac sign to take charge of the start of spring is Aquarius. People are already talking about the beginning of the twenty-first century as being the dawning of the age of Aquarius. But the start of spring will not actually move into Aquarius for another 600 years. This point illustrates that there are many misconceptions about astrology.

Adding in the thirteenth sign

The changes in the star map have allowed a thirteenth star constellation to slip into the zodiac belt – Ophiuchus. The lowest part of this constellation lies between Sagittarius and Scorpio.

This so-called thirteenth zodiac sign has resulted in a flood of new astrology books, which have assigned a fresh set of personality traits to the new sign. It has also been used in other publications in order to denounce the whole idea of astrology.

We don't need to enter into this debate. We will stick with the twelve traditional signs:

- Twelve was chosen by our ancestors because it can be divided into four seasons. It also divides into the 360 degrees of a circle.

- We are only dealing with tendencies, not accurate measurements. If your birth date does not quite fit with your zodiac sign, then it is likely to relate to the one next door. This adjustment is explained in the next chapter.

CHECKLIST OF KEY POINTS

1. The stars appear to be fixed to the celestial sphere over and around the earth.

2. The celestial sphere moves east to west as the earth rotates.

3. The sun moves east to west inside the celestial sphere, following the zodiac belt.

4. The zodiac belt moves a little faster than the sun. This means the sun moves backwards in relation to the zodiac constellations.

5. There are twelve zodiac signs, which form a calendar. It takes exactly a year for the sun to move through all twelve signs.

6. Finding your own birth sign in the night sky is:
   (a) directly experiencing astrology
   (b) best done at a time other than your birthday
   (c) achieved by knowing when and where to look
   (d) assisted by setting up a viewpoint and a distant landmark.

7. There are a number of misconceptions about astrology. For example, the age of Aquarius will not arrive for another 600 years.

CASE STUDIES

Louise has an excellent point of view

The garden of Louise's house backs onto open fields. At the bottom of the garden there is a gate which leads to a footpath. Standing at the gate, Louise uses a magnetic compass to find where south is. It is in the direction of some farm buildings about half a mile across the open fields. She also checks this direction by looking at the position of the sun at midday.

This gives Louise a viewpoint and landmark to help her locate the zodiac signs.

Louise goes out almost every night at 10.p.m., over a period of several months. Although many of the nights are cloudy, her patience is rewarded by being able to see most of the zodiac constellations, including her own, Pisces.

Aquarius brings a new dawn for Elaine

Elaine used to scrape a living by writing romantic fiction. She wrote to a basic formula, and would be the first to admit her stories were uninspired. Elaine's ambition was to write a successful novel, even a bestseller.

Elaine did most of her research in her local library. But a year ago when she was looking for an idea for a new character, she found a book about astrology.

Elaine is an Aquarian who sometimes read her horoscope in the newspaper. She had never really understood, however, what being born under Aquarius meant.

Using the guidance in the astrology book, Elaine was able to locate her own birth sign in the night sky. She began to see herself as a unique individual with her own ideas about life.

Elaine abandoned writing to someone else's formula, and she threw herself into writing a novel inspired by her own thoughts and feelings. After nine months of hard work, she found a publisher eager to take on her new book. Soon after publication, initial sales suggested that this could be the book she had always wanted to write.

3

Finding Your Body and Mind Type

DETERMINING YOUR PROFILE

This chapter will show you how to draw up a personal profile of your body and mind, which consists of a combination of physical and emotional characteristics. The key steps are:

1. Check your personality against the expected profile of your zodiac sign.

2. Then find out if your nervous system is biased left or right.

3. Finally you will compile your personal profile card from the information gathered in steps 1 and 2.

INVESTIGATING PERSONALITY

Let us now see how your personality compares with the twelve traditional zodiac profiles. In the next chapter we will investigate why personality relates to birth date.

Symbolising your personality

In this book, astrology is used at a practical level, in the same way it was used a long time ago, when there were no printed calendars or accurate clocks.

One of the more recent additions is for people to liken their personality to their zodiac symbol. For example, people born within the sign of Libra will tell you that they are just like scales, trying to keep their balance between conflicting demands. In fact, there is no connection between the zodiac symbols and human personality.

The stars are a very long way from the earth and the zodiac constellations do not exert any physical influence on us. They are simply a fixed background against which we gauge the movement and influence of the sun. Technically the zodiac signs should be called the *sun signs*.

The twelve personality profiles which we will look at in this chapter are linked only to the zodiac dates. They are not related to what the symbol is supposed to represent.

Using the scorecards

It is suggested that you photocopy the scorecards, rather than marking them in the book. This will allow you to use them again with your friends and family.

- Score honestly.

- Avoid trying to make the outcome what you would like it to be.

- Don't be disappointed if you get a low score against your own birth sign the first time round.

- Discuss with a friend to help build a more accurate result.

- Be prepared to accept your negative traits as well as the positive side to your personality.

Scoring your personality

Twelve score cards have been provided (see Figures 8 to 19). Each of these is labelled with a zodiac name together with the period of the year it covers.

If you were born in the southern hemisphere you should use the scorecard for six signs ahead of yours. For example, if you were born in Christchurch, New Zealand, on 1 September use the Pisces scorecard not Virgo.

Here are the key steps for completing your scorecard:

1. Select the correct card in which your birth date falls.

2. Start with the group of five tendencies under *emotional*. Tick one box against each description as follows:
   - No tendency for what is described use the nil box.
   - A very strong tendency, use box 5.
   - A weak tendency, use box 1.
   - Somewhere in between, choose which box you think is most appropriate.

3. Add up the total score for *emotional*. For example, if you have ticked the following boxes: 3, 4, 4, 4, 5, then your total score will be: 20.

4. Repeat this exercise for the *thinking* section, then go on to the *relationship* section.

ARIES

21 March – 19 April

Tick one box against each characteristic

Emotional tendencies

	nil	weak				strong
	0	1	2	3	4	5
Competitive and likes to win	☐	☐	☐	☐	☐	☐
Open and honest	☐	☐	☐	☐	☐	☐
Enthusiastic	☐	☐	☐	☐	☐	☐
Optimistic	☐	☐	☐	☐	☐	☐
Does not enjoy trivial jobs	☐	☐	☐	☐	☐	☐

Total score __

Thinking tendencies

	nil	weak				strong
	0	1	2	3	4	5
Careless with details	☐	☐	☐	☐	☐	☐
Sets clear goals	☐	☐	☐	☐	☐	☐
Ideas are vivid, practical and imaginative	☐	☐	☐	☐	☐	☐
Not interested in the politics of the workplace	☐	☐	☐	☐	☐	☐
Looks for opportunities to learn and progress	☐	☐	☐	☐	☐	☐

Total score __

Relationship tendencies

	nil	weak				strong
	0	1	2	3	4	5
Tends to lose interest if not in command	☐	☐	☐	☐	☐	☐
Warm and hospitable	☐	☐	☐	☐	☐	☐
Expects others to follow his or her lead	☐	☐	☐	☐	☐	☐
Uses wit and brains to get what he or she wants	☐	☐	☐	☐	☐	☐
Expects not to be criticised	☐	☐	☐	☐	☐	☐

Total score __

Fig. 8. The Aries scorecard.

TAURUS

20 April – 20 May

Tick one box against each characteristic

Emotional tendencies	nil	weak				strong
	0	1	2	3	4	5
Quiet and unpretentious	☐	☐	☐	☐	☐	☐
Defensive in unexpected situations	☐	☐	☐	☐	☐	☐
Enjoys comfort	☐	☐	☐	☐	☐	☐
Prefers well ordered situations	☐	☐	☐	☐	☐	☐
Able to handle emergencies	☐	☐	☐	☐	☐	☐

Total score __

Thinking tendencies	nil	weak				strong
	0	1	2	3	4	5
Can evaluate a situation quickly	☐	☐	☐	☐	☐	☐
Has practical common sense	☐	☐	☐	☐	☐	☐
Does not make hasty judgements	☐	☐	☐	☐	☐	☐
Sticks to stated principles	☐	☐	☐	☐	☐	☐
Good with money and finance	☐	☐	☐	☐	☐	☐

Total score __

Relationship tendencies	nil	weak				strong
	0	1	2	3	4	5
Loyal to friends	☐	☐	☐	☐	☐	☐
Sensual	☐	☐	☐	☐	☐	☐
Dislikes interference	☐	☐	☐	☐	☐	☐
Dependable	☐	☐	☐	☐	☐	☐
Vulnerable to false affection	☐	☐	☐	☐	☐	☐

Total score __

Fig. 9. The Taurus scorecard.

GEMINI

21 May – 20 June

Tick one box against each characteristic

Emotional tendencies	nil	weak				strong
	0	1	2	3	4	5
Possesses lots of nervous energy	☐	☐	☐	☐	☐	☐
Has a need for emotional warmth	☐	☐	☐	☐	☐	☐
Impatient with mundane tasks	☐	☐	☐	☐	☐	☐
Enjoys fast action and quick returns	☐	☐	☐	☐	☐	☐
Represses strong emotions	☐	☐	☐	☐	☐	☐

Total score __

Thinking tendencies	nil	weak				strong
	0	1	2	3	4	5
Can deal with two things at once	☐	☐	☐	☐	☐	☐
Interested in many things	☐	☐	☐	☐	☐	☐
Notices every detail	☐	☐	☐	☐	☐	☐
Never stops thinking, even during rest	☐	☐	☐	☐	☐	☐
Good generator of new ideas	☐	☐	☐	☐	☐	☐

Total score __

Relationship tendencies	nil	weak				strong
	0	1	2	3	4	5
Friendly and persuasive	☐	☐	☐	☐	☐	☐
Good conversationalist	☐	☐	☐	☐	☐	☐
Finds it hard to ask for emotional warmth	☐	☐	☐	☐	☐	☐
Can appear cool and distant	☐	☐	☐	☐	☐	☐
Finds it difficult to express love	☐	☐	☐	☐	☐	☐

Total score __

Fig. 10. The Gemini scorecard.

CANCER

21 June – 22 July

Tick one box against each characteristic

Emotional tendencies	nil	weak				strong
	0	1	2	3	4	5
Sensitive and emotional	☐	☐	☐	☐	☐	☐
Doesn't push him/herself into limelight	☐	☐	☐	☐	☐	☐
Loves security	☐	☐	☐	☐	☐	☐
Easily hurt	☐	☐	☐	☐	☐	☐
Takes most things very seriously	☐	☐	☐	☐	☐	☐

Total score __

Thinking tendencies	nil	weak				strong
	0	1	2	3	4	5
Rarely acts impulsively	☐	☐	☐	☐	☐	☐
Rarely forgets anything	☐	☐	☐	☐	☐	☐
Good business sense	☐	☐	☐	☐	☐	☐
Tends to use intuition rather than logic	☐	☐	☐	☐	☐	☐
Good at remembering details	☐	☐	☐	☐	☐	☐

Total score __

Relationship tendencies	nil	weak				strong
	0	1	2	3	4	5
Responds to appreciation	☐	☐	☐	☐	☐	☐
Enjoys taking responsibility	☐	☐	☐	☐	☐	☐
Accepts criticism calmly	☐	☐	☐	☐	☐	☐
Has a fear of rejection	☐	☐	☐	☐	☐	☐
Loyal and devoted	☐	☐	☐	☐	☐	☐

Total score __

Fig. 11. The Cancer scorecard.

LEO

Tick one box against each characteristic

Emotional tendencies	nil	weak				strong
	0	1	2	3	4	5
Plenty of mental energy	☐	☐	☐	☐	☐	☐
Strong in emergencies	☐	☐	☐	☐	☐	☐
Self-confident	☐	☐	☐	☐	☐	☐
Mature	☐	☐	☐	☐	☐	☐
Secret doubts about themselves	☐	☐	☐	☐	☐	☐

Total score __

Thinking tendencies	nil	weak				strong
	0	1	2	3	4	5
Use charm to get results	☐	☐	☐	☐	☐	☐
Adventurous often reckless	☐	☐	☐	☐	☐	☐
Dislikes menial tasks	☐	☐	☐	☐	☐	☐
Practical	☐	☐	☐	☐	☐	☐
Good at showing people how to do things	☐	☐	☐	☐	☐	☐

Total score __

Relationship tendencies	nil	weak				strong
	0	1	2	3	4	5
Trusting	☐	☐	☐	☐	☐	☐
Generous with affection	☐	☐	☐	☐	☐	☐
Craves appreciation and recognition	☐	☐	☐	☐	☐	☐
Finds it difficult to tolerate failure	☐	☐	☐	☐	☐	☐
Cold hearted when hurt	☐	☐	☐	☐	☐	☐

Total score __

Fig. 12. The Leo scorecard.

VIRGO

23 August – 22 September

Tick one box against each characteristic

Emotional tendencies	nil	weak				strong
	0	1	2	3	4	5
Unsentimental	☐	☐	☐	☐	☐	☐
Basically shy	☐	☐	☐	☐	☐	☐
Does not express feelings easily	☐	☐	☐	☐	☐	☐
Modest	☐	☐	☐	☐	☐	☐
Strength of purpose	☐	☐	☐	☐	☐	☐

Total score __

Thinking tendencies	nil	weak				strong
	0	1	2	3	4	5
Notices and remembers details	☐	☐	☐	☐	☐	☐
Analyses situations in detail	☐	☐	☐	☐	☐	☐
Orderly and efficient	☐	☐	☐	☐	☐	☐
Courteous and methodical	☐	☐	☐	☐	☐	☐
Likes acquiring information	☐	☐	☐	☐	☐	☐

Total score __

Relationship tendencies	nil	weak				strong
	0	1	2	3	4	5
Helpful to others	☐	☐	☐	☐	☐	☐
Fully committed and loyal	☐	☐	☐	☐	☐	☐
Kind and considerate	☐	☐	☐	☐	☐	☐
Emotionally warm	☐	☐	☐	☐	☐	☐
Likes to take responsibility	☐	☐	☐	☐	☐	☐

Total score __

Fig. 13. The Virgo scorecard.

LIBRA

23 September – 22 October

Tick one box against each characteristic

Emotional tendencies	nil	weak				strong
	0	1	2	3	4	5
Loving and romantic	☐	☐	☐	☐	☐	☐
Sometimes moody	☐	☐	☐	☐	☐	☐
Dislikes being alone	☐	☐	☐	☐	☐	☐
Cares about personal appearance	☐	☐	☐	☐	☐	☐
Sometimes fickle	☐	☐	☐	☐	☐	☐

Total score __

Thinking tendencies	nil	weak				strong
	0	1	2	3	4	5
Good powers of analysis	☐	☐	☐	☐	☐	☐
Likes home/office organised and clean	☐	☐	☐	☐	☐	☐
Good at planning ahead	☐	☐	☐	☐	☐	☐
Likes to spend time thinking before making a decision	☐	☐	☐	☐	☐	☐
Good at promoting ideas	☐	☐	☐	☐	☐	☐

Total score __

Relationship tendencies	nil	weak				strong
	0	1	2	3	4	5
Good listener	☐	☐	☐	☐	☐	☐
Excellent at partnership and teamwork	☐	☐	☐	☐	☐	☐
Rarely unpleasant to others	☐	☐	☐	☐	☐	☐
Takes notice of everyone's opinions	☐	☐	☐	☐	☐	☐
Good mediator	☐	☐	☐	☐	☐	☐

Total score __

Fig. 14. The Libra scorecard.

SCORPIO

23 October – 21 November

Tick one box against each characteristic

Emotional tendencies

	nil	weak				strong
	0	1	2	3	4	5
Keeps thoughts to themselves	☐	☐	☐	☐	☐	☐
Possessive	☐	☐	☐	☐	☐	☐
Single minded	☐	☐	☐	☐	☐	☐
Intense curiosity about others	☐	☐	☐	☐	☐	☐
Gentle towards the weak	☐	☐	☐	☐	☐	☐

Total score __

Thinking tendencies

	nil	weak				strong
	0	1	2	3	4	5
Can solve the most difficult problems	☐	☐	☐	☐	☐	☐
Tenacious	☐	☐	☐	☐	☐	☐
Likes to get to heart of problem	☐	☐	☐	☐	☐	☐
Good memory	☐	☐	☐	☐	☐	☐
Intense concentration	☐	☐	☐	☐	☐	☐

Total score __

Relationship tendencies

	nil	weak				strong
	0	1	2	3	4	5
Demands high standards	☐	☐	☐	☐	☐	☐
Confronts problems directly	☐	☐	☐	☐	☐	☐
Concern for team members	☐	☐	☐	☐	☐	☐
Unlikely to forgive when hurt	☐	☐	☐	☐	☐	☐
Likes to dominate	☐	☐	☐	☐	☐	☐

Total score __

Fig. 15. The Scorpio scorecard.

SAGITTARIUS
21 November – 21 December

Tick one box against each characteristic

Emotional tendencies

	nil	weak				strong
	0	1	2	3	4	5
Acts on impulse	☐	☐	☐	☐	☐	☐
Erratic and hard to tie down	☐	☐	☐	☐	☐	☐
Cheerful	☐	☐	☐	☐	☐	☐
Likes the comfort of a security blanket	☐	☐	☐	☐	☐	☐
Prefers being with people to being alone	☐	☐	☐	☐	☐	☐

Total score __

Thinking tendencies

	nil	weak				strong
	0	1	2	3	4	5
Good memory for facts	☐	☐	☐	☐	☐	☐
Can be forgetful	☐	☐	☐	☐	☐	☐
Interested in many things	☐	☐	☐	☐	☐	☐
Can overlook details	☐	☐	☐	☐	☐	☐
Comes up with creative interpretations	☐	☐	☐	☐	☐	☐

Total score __

Relationship tendencies

	nil	weak				strong
	0	1	2	3	4	5
Can be tactless but never deliberately cruel	☐	☐	☐	☐	☐	☐
Enjoys company	☐	☐	☐	☐	☐	☐
Dislikes being held back by rules	☐	☐	☐	☐	☐	☐
Outspoken	☐	☐	☐	☐	☐	☐
Friendly to people from all walks of life	☐	☐	☐	☐	☐	☐

Total score __

Fig. 16. The Sagittarius scorecard.

CAPRICORN

22 December – 19 January

Tick one box against each characteristic

Emotional tendencies	nil	weak				strong
	0	1	2	3	4	5
Self-conscious	☐	☐	☐	☐	☐	☐
Not interested in being famous	☐	☐	☐	☐	☐	☐
Likes security of routine	☐	☐	☐	☐	☐	☐
Dislikes being teased	☐	☐	☐	☐	☐	☐
Strong willed	☐	☐	☐	☐	☐	☐

Total score __

Thinking tendencies	nil	weak				strong
	0	1	2	3	4	5
Traditional and conventional	☐	☐	☐	☐	☐	☐
Totally reliable in pursuit of an aim	☐	☐	☐	☐	☐	☐
Likes to create things of practical use	☐	☐	☐	☐	☐	☐
Dislikes waste	☐	☐	☐	☐	☐	☐
Tidy and well organised	☐	☐	☐	☐	☐	☐

Total score __

Relationship tendencies	nil	weak				strong
	0	1	2	3	4	5
Get what they want by wearing down resistance	☐	☐	☐	☐	☐	☐
Just one or two close friends	☐	☐	☐	☐	☐	☐
A hard worker	☐	☐	☐	☐	☐	☐
Expects obedience to the rules	☐	☐	☐	☐	☐	☐
Does not mix well	☐	☐	☐	☐	☐	☐

Total score __

Fig. 17. The Capricorn scorecard.

AQUARIUS

20 January – 18 February

Tick one box against each characteristic

Emotional tendencies	nil	weak				strong
	0	1	2	3	4	5
Uncertainty and lack of confidence	☐	☐	☐	☐	☐	☐
Unwilling to reveal feelings	☐	☐	☐	☐	☐	☐
Can be unpredictable	☐	☐	☐	☐	☐	☐
Dislikes emotional tension around them	☐	☐	☐	☐	☐	☐
Appears detached and dispassionate	☐	☐	☐	☐	☐	☐

Total score __

Thinking tendencies	nil	weak				strong
	0	1	2	3	4	5
Inventive	☐	☐	☐	☐	☐	☐
Intuitive thinker with practical streak	☐	☐	☐	☐	☐	☐
Can be absent minded	☐	☐	☐	☐	☐	☐
Brings a fresh approach to tasks	☐	☐	☐	☐	☐	☐
Quick thinker with shrewd analysis	☐	☐	☐	☐	☐	☐

Total score __

Relationship tendencies	nil	weak				strong
	0	1	2	3	4	5
Intense interest in people	☐	☐	☐	☐	☐	☐
Friendly towards everyone	☐	☐	☐	☐	☐	☐
Does not like emotional demands	☐	☐	☐	☐	☐	☐
Enjoys working with people	☐	☐	☐	☐	☐	☐
Finds it difficult to forgive broken promises	☐	☐	☐	☐	☐	☐

Total score __

Fig. 18. The Aquarius scorecard.

PISCES

Tick one box against each characteristic

Emotional tendencies

	nil	weak				strong
	0	1	2	3	4	5
Shy	☐	☐	☐	☐	☐	☐
Not ambitious for fame and fortune	☐	☐	☐	☐	☐	☐
Likes to belong to somewhere or someone	☐	☐	☐	☐	☐	☐
Even tempered	☐	☐	☐	☐	☐	☐
A private person	☐	☐	☐	☐	☐	☐

Total score __

Thinking tendencies

	nil	weak				strong
	0	1	2	3	4	5
A rich imagination	☐	☐	☐	☐	☐	☐
Absorbs information and ideas	☐	☐	☐	☐	☐	☐
A good judge of character	☐	☐	☐	☐	☐	☐
Difficult for others to understand how he or she thinks	☐	☐	☐	☐	☐	☐
Finds it difficult to explain complicated ideas	☐	☐	☐	☐	☐	☐ .

Total score __

Relationship tendencies

	nil	weak				strong
	0	1	2	3	4	5
Warm and sympathetic	☐	☐	☐	☐	☐	☐
Prefers the company of more mature people	☐	☐	☐	☐	☐	☐
Gets emotional involved in most things	☐	☐	☐	☐	☐	☐
Can be a confusing person	☐	☐	☐	☐	☐	☐
Trusting and hospitable	☐	☐	☐	☐	☐	☐

Total score __

Fig. 19. The Pisces scorecard.

Interpreting the results

If you obtain a table score of 15 or more for each of the three tendencies: *emotional, thinking, relationship*, this is a good match. You may describe yourself as being typical of your birthsign.

If the scores are below 15 for one or more of the tendencies, then you should repeat the exercise using an adjacent scorecard. For example if you were born on 21 January, and the Aquarius scorecard gives poor results, try the Capricorn scorecard.

If you have used an adjacent scorecard and you obtain a good match, then you should describe yourself as born in Aquarius but typically Capricorn in personality.

Information on the scorecard that gives the best fit to your personality is used as part of your **personal profile**.

If you have still not been able to obtain a high enough score for your own birth sign, or one of the adjacent signs, then you may find your profile in one of the other more distant signs, or spread across two or more signs.

This means you will have to spend a bit more time going through all the scorecards to try and identify where your personality lies.

IDENTIFYING YOUR BIO-TYPE

You can identify your bio-type using the scorecard in Figure 20. But the scorecard needs to be used with care if the results are to be meaningful. The following points need to be considered:

1. Age and maturity

The scorecard will only work properly with males and females who have passed puberty. Using it with children and adolescents is likely to give false results.

2. State of health

The scorecard statements assume that you are in a normal healthy state. If you are suffering from ill health you may have to look back to a time before your health deteriorated.

3. Stereotypes

When you first look through the scorecard statements, you may be tempted to conclude that the left-biased people tend to be slim and underweight. But many overweight people are left-biased. And there are plenty of slim right-biased people in the world. So it is better to avoid making judgements until you've been through the exercise properly.

4. Menstrual cycle
Women will get a more meaningful result if they use the bio-type scorecard during the early stages of their menstrual cycle.

5. Accuracy
It is relatively easy to identify the strongly left and right-biased people. For those in the middle it becomes less certain. This potential difficulty is dealt with in Chapter 5.

6. There is no best bio-type
You have been built as you are and you can do very little to change that. What does matter is that you adjust your needs to match the kind of person you are. This is a much more practical approach than wishing you were someone else.

7. Scoring honestly
You should score accordingly to what you are – not what you would like to be. For this exercise to work, you must answer the questions about the real you.

Using the bio-type scorecard
There are 20 pairs of statements on the scorecard in Figure 20.

- On the left-hand side, the statements relate to the characteristics of a person whose nervous system is left-biased.

- On the right-hand side, the statements relate to the characteristics of a person whose nervous system is right-biased.

- Between each pair of statements there are five tick boxes labelled as follows:

    L   – strong left-bias
    T/L – tending to a left-bias
    M   – middle – neither left or right-bias
    T/R – tending to a right-bias
    R   – strong right-bias.

Completing the scorecard
The key steps for completing the bio-type scorecard are as follows:

#	Statement	L	T/L	M	T/R	R	Statement
1.	Very jumpy and nervous	☐	☐	☐	☐	☐	Actions are calm, firm and positive
2.	Rarely dreams and/or unable to recall dreams	☐	☐	☐	☐	☐	Dreams frequently often in colour
3.	Likes to make quick decisions	☐	☐	☐	☐	☐	Takes a lot of time over decisions
4.	A lot of get up and go. Can start early in morning	☐	☐	☐	☐	☐	Finds it difficult to get going in the morning
5.	Dislikes loud and/or sudden noises	☐	☐	☐	☐	☐	Can ignore loud noise – not startled by sudden noises
6.	Fatigue sets in early for mental and physical tasks	☐	☐	☐	☐	☐	Can keep going at things for a long time without tiring
7.	Sexually passionate	☐	☐	☐	☐	☐	Uninterested in sex
8	Impatient and irritable	☐	☐	☐	☐	☐	Seldom gets angry
9.	Appetite is easily satisfied	☐	☐	☐	☐	☐	Can eat as much as is placed in front of them
10.	Has strong emotions	☐	☐	☐	☐	☐	Emotionally stable and calm
11.	Very active and rarely still	☐	☐	☐	☐	☐	Relaxed and methodical
12.	Seldom gets depressed, but often feels anxious	☐	☐	☐	☐	☐	Often feels sad or dejected
13.	Sensitive to bright lights and glare	☐	☐	☐	☐	☐	Not bothered by bright light
14.	Can't stand the thought of and having injections	☐	☐	☐	☐	☐	Not concerned at having injections
15.	Feels very warm when you are in close contact	☐	☐	☐	☐	☐	Cold extremities, eg cold feet in bed
16.	Enjoys physical exercise	☐	☐	☐	☐	☐	Dislikes and avoids physical exercise
17.	Feels refreshed after eight hours sleep	☐	☐	☐	☐	☐	Often still feels tired after eight hours sleep
18.	Thick dry hair	☐	☐	☐	☐	☐	Thin silky smooth hair
19.	Rapid and/or irregular breathing	☐	☐	☐	☐	☐	Slow steady breathing
20.	Stomach easily upset by rich food or alcohol	☐	☐	☐	☐	☐	Can eat and drink almost anything without stomach upsets

Column headings: L T/L M T/R R

Fig. 20. The bio-type scorecard.

1. Start with line number one. Judge yourself against the two statements.
   - Place a tick in the **L** box if you are a **very jumpy and nervous person.**
   - But if you are a person whose **actions are calm, firm and positive** then tick the R box.
   - Use **T/L** if being **jumpy** is a tendency without it being a strong characteristic.
   - Use **T/R** if being **calm** is a tendency without it being a strong characteristic.
   - Use **M** if you feel you are in the middle, or you just don't know.

2. Move on down each line. Treat each pair of statements on its own. Try not to compare the line before, and don't alter previous lines until you reach the end.

3. Complete all 20 lines, and tick one box per line.

4. Leave the scorecard for a while and return to it later. Review each line in turn and make any necessary changes.

5. Total up the number of ticks in each column and enter the figures in the totals boxes at the bottom.

Interpreting the results
The results of your bio-type scorecard test are interpreted as follows:

Left-biased nervous system if total of L plus T/L columns is more than total of R plus T/R columns.

Right-biased nervous system if total of R plus T/R columns is more than total of L plus T/L columns.

Strong-bias (left or right) if most of the ticks are in the column next to the questions.

A tendency to a left or right bias if most of the ticks are spread across the two columns between the questions and the M column.

A weak tendency to a left or right bias if ticks appear in the middle column and on both sides, but with slightly more on one side than the other.

By studying the totals at the bottom of the scorecard, and the distribution of ticks, you will be able to describe your own bio-type. For example: 'I have a nervous system that is tending towards a right bias.'

Measuring your metabolic rate

Metabolism is the process which extracts nutrients from your food, for energy and other body functions – for example, keeping your bones and teeth in good order. The speed at which your digestive process works is called your **metabolic rate**. If you have a left biased nervous system, then it is likely you have a **fast metabolism**. A right bias is associated with **slow metabolism**. The majority of people living in the UK have a slow metabolism. There are different dietary needs associated with the two types of metabolism (discussed in Chapter 5). It is therefore important that you use the bio-type scorecard carefully, so that the results are accurate.

WRITING UP YOUR PERSONAL PROFILE

You can now bring the results from your zodiac and bio-type scorecards together – recording the details on a personal profile card.

The layout of a suitable personal profile card is illustrated in Figure 21. This has been filled in with typical details as an example. You can draw up your own card by hand or on a personal computer, using this layout as a guide.

Completing your profile

Your zodiac scorecard tells you about your emotional make up. The bio-type scorecard is mainly about how your body works. But the bio-type scorecard does include an emotional element.

The steps for filling in the personal profile card are as follows:

1. Write in your name at the top. Then add your nervous system bias, from your interpretation of the scorecard results.

2. From your bio-type scorecard, write in three statements based on how you marked questions 1, 10 and 12. These relate to your emotional make up. They will not necessarily all be the same

strength. It is also possible to have one on the opposite side to the others.

3. From your zodiac scorecard (the one that gave the best match) write in your strongest tendencies, under the three main headings of: emotional, thinking and relationships. Only include those with a score of three or more.

Testing personality

Personality tests are commercially available in book and computer form. They are often called psychometric tests. Usually you can only be tested by people who have been trained. These tests are used by many companies to produce personal profile cards, similar to the one in this book.

Personal profile for _Andrew_

Nervous system bias _Strong right_

1. Emotions

   (a) Bio-type (scorecard questions 1, 10, 12)
   Calm, firm & positive
   Emotionally stable
   Tendency to be sad & dejected

   (b) Zodiac
   Not interested in being famous
   Likes security of routine
   Strong willed

2. Thinking

   Totally reliable in pursuit of an aim
   Likes to create things of practical use
   Tidy & well organised

3. Relationships

   Just one or two friends
   A hard worker
   Expects obedience to the rules
   Does not mix well

Fig. 21. Example of a completed personal profile card.

If you get the opportunity to try a psychometric test, you should find a good match between those results and your own results using the scorecards in this book.

CHECKLIST OF KEY POINTS

Finding your body and mind type
1. Your personality can be checked against the expected profile of your zodiac sign.

2. Your nervous system bias can be determined using a scorecard which includes: behaviour, energy levels and sleep patterns.

3. Your complete personal profile is written up from the information provided from the zodiac and bio-type exercises – and recorded on a personal profile card.

CASE STUDIES

David takes the first step to well-being
David is a financial auditor for a large national company. His work takes him all over the country, and he often has to stay away from home in hotels.

David is in his late 40s and married with two children. He has always been a slim, nervous type of person. And he does tend to suffer from stomach upsets.

More recently, David's stomach problems have got much worse. And he has also put on a lot of weight around his middle. David has tried to cut down on coffee, which he thinks is causing his stomach problems. And he has tried to reduce his consumption of fast foods, which he eats, to save time while on the road.

David has written out a personal profile card. He is strongly left-biased and has all the characteristics of a Gemini. He knows there will be further action he can take to improve his well-being. He has made a start by finding out what kind of person he is. The next step will be to identify his needs.

Lizanne checks up on her doubts
Lizanne is the senior sales person at a furniture warehouse that specialise in supplying fitted kitchens, bedrooms and bathrooms. She has direct contact with customers, helping them to design room

layouts and choose the right pieces of furniture.

Lizanne has the personality of a typical Leo. She is confident and mature, practical and good at showing people what to do. She is also proud of her calm approach, even when dealing with difficult customers.

Lizanne, however, has doubts about herself. She wonders if this calm, confident person is the real Lizanne, or just an image she has created.

A bio-type test provides the answer. Lizanne finds that her nervous system has a bias that is tending to the right. This confirms that she is typically Leo – calm and steady.

Andrew builds for the future

Andrew is in his late 40s, married with two teenage children. He has a passion for building scale model steam locomotives, and spends most of his spare time in his well-equipped workshop.

Andrew's wife, Susan, has been concerned about her relationship with Andrew for some time. She feels that she must be the reason why he wants to spend so much time on his own.

After researching Andrew's zodiac personality, however, Susan is much happier. Andrew, it appears, is a typical Capricorn, thus explaining his strong creative streak, and the tidy, well-organised workshop.

Andrew's bio-type enhances the picture further. Andrew is strongly right-biased. This explains his calm, methodical approach.

Susan learns to accept Andrew as he is and their relationship greatly improves as a result. She starts to take an interest in his model building and Andrew shares with her his long-term plans for selling the finished locomotives to American and Far Eastern buyers.

4

Living with Daylight

SOAKING UP THE SUN

During the period in which the human species evolved from its ape ancestors natural daylight had an important influence on what kind of animal we became. In this chapter we will see why daylight continues to be one of our most important needs.

Taking in vitamins

Vitamins are essential to life.

Key facts about vitamins
1. Vitamins are identified by single letters, for example: A, B, C.

2. The majority of vitamins cannot be made by our bodies.

3. We obtain vitamins by eating plants, or eating animals that have previously eaten plants.

4. Some vitamins can be stored by our bodies, others need to be replaced daily.

5. A deficiency of a vitamin can result in an impairment of a normal body process, illness, or even death.

6. Vitamin deficiency is the most common reason for people becoming unwell.

Letting the sun shine in
The sun is responsible for producing one of the vitamins we require to maintain a healthy life. Vitamin D is produced by the action of

sunlight on our skin. We can obtain vitamin D in some foods of animal origin, but the natural way is to use sunlight.

When our ancestors were apes, the only exposed skin surfaces were the face and part of the hands. This remains the situation today, only we have substituted clothes for the body hair.

The amount of sunlight received depends on where you are on the surface of the earth. Near the equator, where sunlight is very strong, people have evolved with dark skins, which are built-in sun screens.

Eskimos living in the Arctic are so far north that they don't get enough sunlight. The long hours of darkness in the winter is one problem. Then in the summer, the sun is very low and the sunlight is weak. But the food available in this part of the world is very rich in vitamin D, which makes up for the sunlight deficiency.

Living with vitamin D

Vitamin D in our bodies is responsible for pushing calcium and phosphorus into the bloodstream. This process is essential to maintain healthy bones, nerves and muscles.

The following are some key points about sunlight and vitamin D requirements.

- Some people may not be spending enough time outside in natural daylight to meet their vitamin D requirements.

- We have been designed by nature to generate enough vitamin D using the sunlight received on our face and hands. (Sunbathing is discussed later in this chapter.)

- Atmospheric pollution in cities, and shadows from tall buildings, cuts our levels of received sunlight quite dramatically.

- After the age of 40, there is a steady decline in the skin's ability to produce vitamin D. So older people should have more sunlight than younger people.

- Dark skinned people, with ancestors from low latitudes, but who are living in high latitude countries like the United Kingdom, are likely to be short of vitamin D.

Plotting sunlight levels

Figure 22 shows the variation in sunlight for places around 50 degrees north, for example London. The year has been divided up into the zodiac constellations. Using the zodiac or astrological calendar is convenient because:

- It is a fixed *ruler* in the sky, against which we can plot the position of the sun.

- With twelve equal divisions, and because it marks the start of spring *etc*, it links directly with daylight levels.

- It can be used to explain why people have different astrological personalities.

- When dealing with trends and tendencies a simple division of twelve periods is sufficient. There is no need to indicate days and hours.

For the southern hemisphere, the same graph applies, but it needs to be shifted forwards by six of the zodiac periods. This is the reason why the adjustment is made for personality assessment for those born in the southern hemisphere.

Plotting the rise and fall of vitamin D

There can sometimes be higher sunlight levels in July and August, when it is less cloudy. It is also usually warmer in these months.

The graph in Figure 22 is only to demonstrate the ups and downs of daylight and is not intended to give accurate measurements. But you can link the rise and fall of vitamin D directly to it. The second line on the graph shows vitamin D levels in the body.

Vitamin D levels rise and fall in response to sunlight levels. But this response lags behind, because since vitamin D is one of the vitamins that is stored by the body, the body takes a while to store up or lose it.

Adjusting your lifestyle

Most of us spend a lot more time indoors during the day than our bodies intended. This means we are likely to be short of vitamin D. Trying to spend more time outside is a good idea. Hobbies such as gardening and fishing will help. A holiday abroad in a sunny country is also beneficial, particularly during the winter months.

Vitamin D is likely to be at its lowest in the spring. Fish oil capsules, which are a good source of vitamin D, can be used to make up for any shortfalls. But the link between sunlight and vitamin D is only half the story. In addition to the effects that sunlight has on the

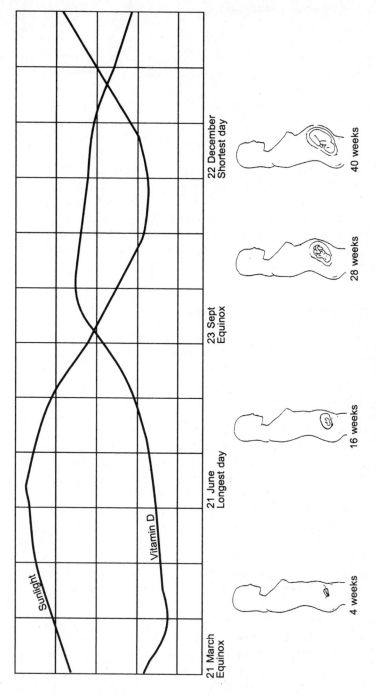

Fig. 22. Sunlight and vitamin D levels.

Sunlight

Vitamin D

21 March
Equinox

21 June
Longest day

23 Sept
Equinox

22 December
Shortest day

4 weeks

16 weeks

28 weeks

40 weeks

skin, there is a link with the endocrine nervous system. We will be looking at this other relationship with daylight later in the chapter.

Giving birth to personality

Under the graphs of sunlight and vitamin D, illustrated in Figure 22, are four stages of development of an unborn child. This child has been conceived in the middle of Aries. It will be born in Capricorn.

During the pregnancy, the foetus grows at a rate more rapid than any other tissue in the human body. And the developing child receives nutrients directly from the mother through the placenta.

The variation in vitamin D levels during the pregnancy is one possible influence on the personality of that child. A child conceived at a different time, and born during a different zodiac period, would be subjected to a different pattern of vitamin D levels.

RECEIVING THE RIGHT SIGNALS

We have seen how sunlight is responsible for the generation of vitamin D. But before we find out how sunlight affects us in other ways, let us have a look at what sunlight is.

Tuning in to the sun

The sun throws out an enormous amount of energy in the form of electromagnetic radiation, which is the same as a radio signal.

The electromagnetic spectrum is illustrated in Figure 23. It includes such familiar names as X-rays and microwaves. The spectrum in Figure 23, however, is nowhere near to scale but is drawn only to show the order of each band of radiation.

Radiation types are identified by their wavelength, which is the distance between two adjacent wave peaks. For example if you are listening to Radio 4 on the longwave band, the wavelength is 1500 metres.

Wavelengths for visible light are extremely small. They are measured in nanometres (nm) which is just one millionth of a millimetre.

Sheltering from ultraviolet

The radiation bands below visible light are called **near ultraviolet** and **far ultraviolet**. Far ultraviolet is usually referred to as **UV-C**. When people talk about the dangers of exposure to ultraviolet, they are usually talking about UV-C.

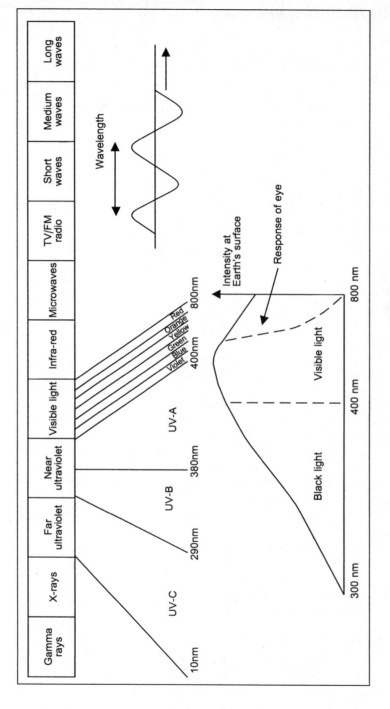

Fig. 23. The electromagnetic spectrum.

65

Practically no UV-C reaches the surface of the earth.

UV-C is lethal to all forms of plant and animal life.

The following are some key points about life on earth and UV-C:

1. A layer of ozone in the upper atmosphere blocks UV-C and prevents it reaching the earth.

2. The ozone layer has been damaged by man-made chemicals, notably refrigerator coolants called CFCs.

3. There is confusion between global warming and ozone layer damage. Global warming is a climate change due to heat being trapped by increasing levels of carbon dioxide gas – known as the greenhouse effect.

Understanding near ultraviolet

Near ultraviolet radiation does reach the earth. This is just a continuation of the visible part of the spectrum, and is sometimes called black light because you can't see it. The relative intensities of near ultraviolet and visible light is shown as a curve at the bottom of the diagram, illustrated in Figure 23.

Near ultraviolet is divided into two bands: **UV-A** and **UV-B**. UV-B is much more powerful than UV-A, but much less UV-B than UV-A reaches the earth. While these technical details need not concern you, you need to be aware that some light tubes that are used in solariums for tanning generate unnaturally high and unbalanced levels of UV-A and UV-B and therefore are dangerous.

The most noticeable effects of near ultraviolet on the human body are:

- the production of vitamin D
- sunburn and suntan.

Shading your eyes

Glass in our windows shuts out almost all the near ultraviolet. So sitting behind your patio doors in full sunlight will neither produce vitamin D nor give you a tan.

Transparent plastic allows most of the near ultraviolet through.

This includes clear spectacle lenses and contact lenses. Many modern lenses are tinted or coated, specifically to block near ultraviolet. Sunglasses also block near ultraviolet as well as reduce the level of the visible light.

The reasons why there is a desire to prevent near ultraviolet reaching the eyes are as follows:

1. Experiments suggest that prolonged exposure to near ultraviolet light can result in eye defects such as cataracts.

2. Near ultraviolet is often associated with UV-C and the fears about ozone layer damage.

3. A great deal more near ultraviolet is being received directly by our eyes, because of reflections. This is as a result of:

   – tarmac and concrete road and pavement surfaces
   – snow, when taking part in winter sports activities or mountaineering
   – agricultural land which has been created by the removal of trees.

Point number 3 is important. Snow reflects a high proportion of near ultraviolet, and we know this leads to snow-blindness. Receiving near ultraviolet directly into the eyes as a result of strong reflections can be as dangerous as looking directly at the sun.

Blocking out near ultraviolet
There is a strong case for blocking out near ultraviolet from the eyes. There is also a strong case, however, for allowing it in. The key points are:

1. The sensitivity of the human eye almost matches the curve of the full spectrum, including the near ultraviolet. So this suggests near ultraviolet is there for a purpose.

2. There is a proven link between the eyes and the endocrine nervous system, which appears to be driven by near ultraviolet.

The above points suggest that the human species has evolved with a requirement for near ultraviolet. This could mean, therefore, that it is unhealthy to shut it out.

COUNTING THE DAYLIGHT HOURS

Tuning in to daylight

Let's first of all deal with how we see. Light enters our eyes through the transparent pupil, and is focused by a lens onto the retina at the back of the eye. The retina converts the light into electrical signals, which are sent along the optic nerve to the brain.

Because light is electromagnetic waves, the light our eyes receive is the same as an AM radio signal. The eye, up to the retina, is the aerial which picks up the signals. The retina through to the brain is a radio receiver, which unscrambles the information carried by the signal.

Linking to the nervous system

In Chapter 1, we saw how the pituitary gland controls the endocrine nervous system, by receiving instructions from the brain.

The connection between the brain and the pituitary is through the lower part of the brain, called the **hypothalamus**, located just above the pituitary. Figure 24 illustrates the link between the hypothalamus and the pituitary.

The hypothalamus sends instructions to the pituitary using hormones, but it receives instructions from other parts of the brain by electrical signals. The hypothalamus can be thought of as being similar to the motorised valve in a domestic central heating system. The valve receives electrical signals from the timer, which tells it to direct the water to the radiators or to the storage tank.

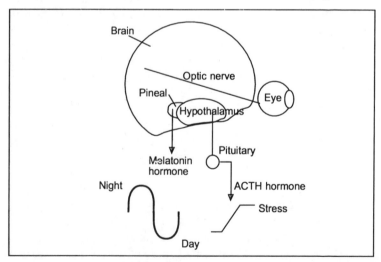

Fig. 24. The hypothalamus, pituitary and pineal.

Running from danger

Your eyes connect to a part of the brain called the visual cortex. The eye and the optic nerve have been included in the diagram illustrated in Figure 24.

If we see something that threatens our safety, part of the reaction is that the hypothalamus instructs the pituitary to release a hormone called ACTH. When ACTH reaches our adrenal glands, cortisone is released. This in turn results in plenty of glucose being available, to give you the energy for a quick getaway.

This is part of what is called the **stress reaction**. It is a good example of how the outside world and our nervous system interact. This also implies that the thinking part of the brain may in some circumstances be able to influence the workings of our bodies. The autonomic nervous system, therefore, is not one hundred per cent automatic.

Seeing with our third eye

The **pineal** is a gland which is attached to the hypothalamus. The pineal is sometimes called **the third eye**, because it is sensitive to light. It is situated well inside our heads, so it can't be influenced directly by the light outside. It appears to be connected to our eyes by at least one, or possibly two, roundabout routes.

In evolutionary terms, the pineal pre-dates our eyes, and our ability to see. It was probably used just to detect night and day.

Feeling SAD

The pineal responds to near ultraviolet light. When we are in darkness the pineal releases a hormone called melatonin but in daylight the hormone production stops.

If you spend long periods away from natural daylight, you can start to feel very depressed. This condition is known as seasonal affective disorder, usually abbreviated to SAD. Its existence implies that we all need a daily dose of natural daylight.

Given the importance of daylight to our well-being, consider the points below.

1. If we are deficient in daylight for long periods, then we may be pushing ourselves around the cycle of unbalance and recovery, which was discussed in Chapter 1 and illustrated in Figure 2.

2. Home and office lighting is the same as darkness as far as the pineal is concerned.

3. Wearing glasses or lenses that block near ultraviolet is the same as putting yourself into perpetual darkness.

4. People have different tolerance levels for different deficiencies and excesses. Some people will need more daylight than others, to maintain their correct balance point and feel well.

Understanding the benefits of daylight

The link between daylight and vitamin D production is a proven scientific fact. The need for daylight, *ie* visible light plus near ultraviolet via our eyes, is based on observation and reasoning.

People who lobby for daylight are certain that:

Natural daylight is essential for human health. It has access to, and influence over, our endocrine nervous system.

The *claimed* benefits of allowing near ultraviolet into our bodies through our eyes are as follows:

1. As sunlight levels increase, the body is told to allow for increased skin pigmentation. This means you suntan rather than sunburn.

2. Our nervous system is better able to fight infections.

3. We are less likely to suffer from many of the degenerative illnesses, such as arthritis.

Many of the ideas about the need for natural daylight came from an American, John Ott. He was a professional photographer, who specialised in time-lapse films, the painstaking process of filming the growth of plants, and condensing it into just a few minutes.

John Ott came to his conclusions about the important of daylight after years of observing plants and animals.

His case is supported by the following points:

1. The proven action of the pineal and the hormone melatonin.

2. Animal breeders who manipulate the quality of light in breeding sheds to improve results.

3. Egg producers who perform similar lighting tricks in chicken sheds to increase egg production.

4. Studies of hormone levels in the blood of people with visual defects.

5. There needs to be a link to daylight for animals to know when to breed.

Later in this chapter, suggestions will be given for a compromise approach for dealing with daylight. This will take into account the potential dangers of overexposure to near ultraviolet, and the potential benefits from receiving natural daylight.

Throwing light on personality types

There are two linked but separate daylight influences that have an effect on our minds and bodies:

(a) the production of vitamin D due to sunlight on our skin, and
(b) changes to hormone levels due to the action of the pineal gland.

These link to the two lines on the graph, illustrated in Figure 22. And because the two influences are not in step, the net effect on an unborn child in the womb is likely to be complex. This offers a reasonable explanation of why each person is born with a personality that relates to date of birth. And why personality is significantly different between people born at different times of the year.

Making use of the sun

The glass in windows blocks most of the near ultraviolet light, but plastic materials allow most of it through. The polycarbonate roofs of modern conservatories, for example, are not completely transparent to near ultraviolet, but a significant amount gets through.

In a conservatory, you can take full advantage of being in natural daylight, while still being indoors.

Here are some key points about the conservatory:

1. Heat it with a hot water radiator connected to the house central heating system, or use an electric convector. You should heat it, so that it can be used all year.

2. Windows need opening top vents to allow for adequate ventilation during hot weather.

3. There is usually plenty of near ultraviolet around, even on dull days and in the winter.

4. The rules about sunbathing and wearing sunglasses, given at the end of this chapter, also apply inside your conservatory.

5. Use your conservatory as a living area, and count the hours you spend in it as if you were outside.

Managing sunlight with trees
Deciduous trees help to manage sunlight naturally.

1. They provide shade in summer, reducing the level of near ultraviolet reflected from pavements and road surfaces.

2. They lose their leaves in winter to allow the weaker sunlight through.

3. The leaf colour is restful to our visual senses because it is in the middle of the colour spectrum.

4. They convert the carbon dioxide we breathe out into oxygen for us to breathe in.

Trees should be planted anywhere they can be fitted in, but particularly:

- around all buildings, including public buildings, schools and supermarkets
- along streets, road and motorways
- in gardens
- around and within car parks
- in the corners of, and around the edges of, fields
- to create coppices – that is small pockets of managed woodland where the wood is harvested by thinning the trees periodically.

WORKING WITH ARTIFICIAL LIGHT

It is possible to produce lighting which emulates natural daylight, including near ultraviolet. This is called **full spectrum lighting**.

The type of lighting we live and work under tends to be chosen by cost. Most people go for lights that are cheap to buy and which consume as little power as possible. The *quality* of the light that is produced, and how it might be affecting our health, is rarely considered.

Making artificial light
We use two main types of light source:

1. Incandescent
Incandescent lighting is what is predominantly used in domestic situations.

- It is inefficient, with most of the energy coming out as heat rather than light.

- The light peaks towards the red end of the visible spectrum. This has the advantage of making rooms looks warmer.

- Daylight bulbs are available. These have a blue coating inside the glass bulb, to shift the colour towards the blue end of the spectrum. They are designed for specialist use, for example, for artists who want daylight conditions in their studios.

2. Fluorescent
Fluorescent lighting is used extensively in industrial and office situations, and is more efficient and cheaper to run than incandescent lights. It consists of a tube of mercury vapour through which an electric charge is passed. (Sodium is used in the orange street lights.) Ultraviolet is produced, which is absorbed by a powder coating on the inside of the tube. The powder glows, as a result of the ultraviolet energy, giving off visible light.

- Different types of powder coating can be used to give different ranges of light, including colours.

- Sunbeds in solariums use tubes that have been specially made to emit UV-A and UV-B, often at a much higher intensity than you will receive through natural sunlight.

Working under fluorescent lighting

A small number of people are noticeably affected when they work under fluorescent lighting. They may suffer from one or more of the following:

- headaches
- migraines
- difficulty in concentration
- a feeling of tension
- nausea
- fatigue.

Some studies have shown that prolonged exposure to artificial light can increase the level of the stress hormone ACTH.

Refer back to Figure 24. Because of the link between the eyes and the pituitary, through the hypothalamus, it is possible that poor quality light might cause ACTH to be released. In some people, this may be quite significant, causing them to feel unwell.

Feeling sick inside buildings

It is a recognised phenomenon that some office buildings have a detrimental effect on people, making them feel unsettled and unhappy, even unwell. It is known as the **sick building syndrome**.

Artificial lighting may be one contributing factor. Others may include:

- air conditioning systems
- static electric charges from carpets
- stressful style of accommodation (see Chapter 6 for a fuller discussion of this).

If you feel uncomfortable when working under fluorescent lights, there are a number of ways of ameliorating the situation.

- When you are dealing with paperwork, use a desklamp fitted with an incandescent bulb. This will swamp out the effects of the more distant fluorescent lighting. Fitting a daylight bulb may improve the situation further.

- Ask an optician to supply you with a pair of glasses with blue tinted lenses. The blue tint inside the glass of a daylight bulb is a useful guide to the sort of colour you will need. If you don't require any vision correction, blue tinted plain lenses are all you need. Often people who experience difficulties in artificial light, think there is something wrong with their eyes, even though their vision is quite normal.

• Plastic sheets placed over papers on a desk can also be used to reduce reflected light. Clear plastic is often adequate. You can also experiment with different colours to find which produces the most restful situation. Clear and coloured plastic sheets are available from office suppliers in the form of A4 and A3 plastic sleeves for filing papers.

Coping with computers

Whether we like it or not, personal computers are here to stay. Many of us have jobs that involve spending long periods of time looking at a computer screen.

The light reaching our eyes from a computer screen is artificial. This may mean that our nervous system is placed under stress, in the same way as working in fluorescent light. The people who are affected by lighting are also likely to be affected in a similar way, when working with a PC.

It is worth mentioning here that we are discussing PCs with cathode ray tube display screens – similar to television sets. The flat screens that are inside the fold-out tops of lap-top PCs work differently. They are liquid crystal with lights behind. The light levels are much lower than with the TV style display screens. Flat screens are less likely to cause people visual stress but the advice given below can still be usefully applied to flat screens too.

Regulating computers

The use of computers at work is controlled by the Display Screen Equipment (DSE) regulations. The regulations cover statutory breaks, the siting of equipment to avoid reflections, the correct height of chairs and keyboards and so on.

The following important points should be noted. These apply to all computer users, not just to those who feel the screens are causing them stress.

1. Always stick to DSE rules. Take the statutory breaks, usually 15 minutes in the morning and in the afternoon.

2. Ensure the screen is at the right height for you, and that your chair is adjusted correctly. Your company should have a copy of

the DSE regulations so that you can check your operating position. Your company may also have their own publication covering DSE work. Make sure you read and understand these.

3. Employers should have their sites arranged so that it is easy for employers to take DSE and lunch breaks. Ideally a conservatory area should be provided, so that employees can have their breaks in natural daylight.

Changing colour

Blue-tinted glasses are also useful for PC users.

It is possible with most PCs to change the colour of the background and text. But you may need to experiment with different combinations, so that all the other general computer instructions on the screen are still readable.

To reduce glare, it is better to have a dark background with a light text, which is opposite to the usual screen displays. Changes are made via the operating system (*eg* Windows). The background is usually referred to as the *window*, and the text as the *font*. If you are unsure of how to do this, ask a friend or colleague who is familiar with PCs. One of the most restful colour combinations is a green text on a black background.

Minimising magnetism

Sitting in front of a computer screen for lengthy periods can also create another problem. It is possible for the electromagnetic radiation to magnetise the iron in your red blood cells, causing the cells to clump together. This can result in headaches, nausea, fatigue and eyestrain. To relieve this difficulty, a period outside in natural daylight will allow the blood cells to return to their natural pattern.

TAKING THE RIGHT DOSE OF DAYLIGHT

The right dose of natural daylight needs to be a sensible compromise between:

- Deficiency – which may result in:

  - insufficient vitamin D production
  - increased stress
  - seasonal affective disorder (SAD)

	Do	Try to	Try not to	Avoid	Don't
Living in daylight	Have a daily dose of daylight	Take part in outdoor activities, eg gardening, walking, football	Work through statutory computer & lunch breaks at work	Wearing sunglasses or UV blocking lenses outside, except in situations with strong reflections, eg snow	Allow your vitamin D level to drop through lack of daylight
Tanning your skin	Use an appropriate sun screen cream if you must lie out in the sun	Get your tan doing activities other than formal sunbathing eg working in the garden	Wear sunglasses or UV blocking lenses	Roasting yourself for hours on end	Visit a solarium or use a sunbed
Shading your eyes	Wear sunglasses when driving (the windscreen glass will have already blocked the UV)	Restrict the use of sunglasses or UV blocking lenses to difficult situations eg snow, dry grassland	Wear sunglasses or UV blocking lenses when trying to get a suntan	Wearing sunglasses or tinted lenses purely as a fashion accessory	Miss out on beneficial UV by using permanently tinted or UV blocking lenses

Fig. 25. Daylight guidelines.

- potential for degenerative illness
- less ability to fight infections.

• Excess - which may result in:

  - eye damage
  - skin problems.

A practical compromise is summarised in Figure 25.

CHECKLIST OF KEY POINTS

Vitamin D

1. Produced by the action of near ultraviolet on the skin of the face and the hands.

2. Production varies according to latitude and colour of skin.

3. Can be obtained from food, especially fish, to make up a deficiency due to lack of sunlight.

4. Many people may not be getting enough sunlight to produce their requirements.

5. Levels can be plotted against the time of year - they are lowest in the spring.

6. Variation in levels may have an influence on astrological personality.

Ultraviolet

1. Sunlight is electromagnetic radiation - the same as a radio signal.

2. Far ultraviolet, or UV-C, is blocked by the ozone layer in the earth's atmosphere, and it does not reach the earth's surface.

3. UV-C is lethal to all forms of life.

4. Near ultraviolet (UV-A and UV-B) does reach the earth's surface.

5. Near ultraviolet is responsible for: vitamin D production, suntan and sunburn.

6. Glass and tinted lenses block out near ultraviolet. Plastic materials allow it to pass.

7. Our eyes can receive too much near ultraviolet because of reflections from snow and hard surfaces.

Daylight and our nervous system
1. The brain is responsible for seeing.

2. The brain connects to the pituitary gland via the hypothalamus.

3. If we see danger, the pituitary releases the hormone ACTH. This is part of the stress reaction.

4. The pineal gland is light sensitive. When we are in darkness, it releases the hormone melatonin.

5. Long periods away from daylight can cause seasonal affective disorder (SAD).

6. There is a strong case to support the connection between daylight and health.

7. Near ultraviolet, and its link to the nervous system, may be a contributor to zodiac personality, in conjunction with vitamin D levels.

8. A conservatory with a plastic roof will allow you to take advantage of natural daylight indoors.

9. Trees are the natural way to manage sunlight.

Artificial light
1. Artificial light is usually either incandescent or fluorescent.

2. A small number of people are noticeably affected while working in artificial light.

3. Too much artificial light may cause stress to your nervous system.

4. Lighting may be a contributor to sick building syndrome.

5. You can take action to reduce the stressful effects of artificial light, for example with tinted glasses.

6. Working with computer screens can also cause difficulties, but changing the colour of your computer display will make it easier to work with.

CASE STUDIES

Rashid solves his vitamin D deficiency

Rashid is a computer maintenance engineer with a large banking organisation. His work involves travelling to branches throughout the Midlands, to service computer systems and offer assistance to the users. He travels by car, and during his working hours spends virtually no time outside in daylight.

Rashid is a member of his local cricket team, which means he is outside at weekends and evenings during the summer months.

Although he is young and in relatively good health, Rashid sometimes suffers from aches in his joints and the occasional attack of cramp. This always seems to be worse in the spring, and he finds it hard to get going at the beginning of the cricket season.

Rashid wonders whether perhaps he is not getting enough sunlight. He is Asian with a dark skin, which means he is not very efficient at producing vitamin D. He takes fish oil capsules, from the beginning of March through to the end of June. Consequently he finds that his joints improve and when the new cricket season opens, his performance improves also.

Alison brings the sunshine indoors

We have already met Alison in a case study at the end of Chapter 1. She is unhappy at work, thinks she is developing arthritis, and yearns for a holiday in the sun.

Alison's husband has just finished building a conservatory at the back of their house. They furnish it with a dining table and chairs, plus a couple of lounge chairs. The conservatory is heated and can be used at any time of the year.

Alison starts having breakfast in the conservatory before going to work. It is also used by her and the family for their evening meals. Alison makes sure she takes the statutory breaks at work, away from her computer, and she tries to use part of her 45 minute lunch break to go for a short walk each day.

On Saturdays, Alison and her husband avoid using enclosed shopping centres. And on Sundays, if they are not working in their own garden, they try to go for a walk at their local country park.

Within only a few weeks, Alison starts to feel much better. She is no longer depressed and the pains in her joints have improved significantly.

A refreshing change of colour for Jason

Jason has been a manger in an engineering company for over ten years. Recently the offices have been upgraded, and all the work transferred from paper plans and specifications to a computer system.

Jason is slightly long-sighted and has always used reading glasses when dealing with paperwork. But under the new office lighting and when working with his computer, Jason thinks his eyes have suddenly deteriorated. He is getting headaches and often feels quite sick by the end of the day.

His optician has dealt with this kind of problem before. He makes Jason a pair of reading glasses with a pale blue tint, and advises him to buy a desk lamp and fit a daylight bulb. He suggests also that he tries a different combination of colours for his computer screen. These changes do result in an immediate improvement, and Jason is able to work comfortably in the new office environment.

5

Achieving a Balance

REVIEWING THE SITUATION

In Chapter 1 we introduced the idea that you have a balance point. This is when the needs of your body and mind are matched by what your surroundings have to offer.

Getting out of balance

Getting out of balance will happen if you receive excesses, or are deficient in essentials that you do need. Either of these situations can result in you:

- feeling unwell
- putting on weight
- becoming unhappy
- experiencing difficulties with relationships
- growing uncertain about your role in life.

Noticing something is wrong

The effects of excesses or deficiencies may not be noticed right away. What happens is shown in the unbalance and recovery cycle, illustrated in Figure 2. The body and mind will fight back for some time. This is the **adaption stage**.

But if the excess or deficiency continues, you will be pushed into the **exhaustion stage**. It is only then that you will notice something is wrong. What happens will depend on your personality and bio-type, but in all cases, the tendencies are negative:

- Positive characteristics will be blunted. *Example*: a quick thinker will find it more difficult to make decisions.

- Negative characteristics will become more negative. *Example*: a shy person will become more withdrawn.

- The digestive system will be less able to handle many types of food. *Example*: you start to put on weight, even though you have not changed your diet.

Important note
How you put on weight can depend on your bio-type. As a general rule, people with left-biased nervous systems gain weight on the waist and torso and people with right-biased systems gain weight on hips and thighs.

Taking action to put things right
Before you can take action to put things right, you need to look for the root causes of your problems. Attacking the symptoms will achieve very little. You need to find out what has pushed you off balance, in order to make an effective recovery. But before that, you need to understand what your needs are, to achieve a proper body and mind balance.

COUNTING CALORIES

Let us look at a simple explanation of how our bodies process food. This will help us to understand why things can often go wrong, and why there is a lot of truth in the old saying: 'One man's meat is another man's poison.'

Processing your food
We can think of our bodies as a machine with two main parts:

1. The **processing** part produces
    – energy to allow us to move and think
    – heat to maintain body temperature
    and extracts material for building and maintenance, *eg* calcium for our bones.

2. The **control** part
    – works via the endocrine nervous system
    – regulates energy production using the right side of the brain
    – manages building and maintenance using the left side of the brain.

Because the processing is controlled by the left and right side of the brain, this means that different bio-types process their food in different ways. One is better at extracting energy, the other is better at building and maintaining.

They each have different experiences of physical problems,

including putting on weight. Consequently any unbalance can only be put right by taking action that is appropriate to the needs of the bio-type. So different bio-types need to use different diets to lose weight.

Taking in the essentials
It will help us later in this chapter, if we take a look at what goes into our bodies and what comes out.

Food and water
The fuel to power our bodies, and the body building elements, are contained in our food.

Oxygen
Pure unpolluted air consists of a mixture of:

Nitrogen	78 per cent
Oxygen	21 per cent
Other gases	1 per cent

Other gases include carbon dioxide, inert gases like argon, plus small traces of methane and hydrogen. Ozone, which is so important in the upper atmosphere as a screen against UV-C, is only present in minute quantities at ground level (0.0005%).

Our bodies only use the oxygen, which is absorbed by our lungs and transferred to our blood stream.

Sensory messages
Feeding into the control part of the processing machine are all the messages from our senses. Here are two examples of how our senses can affect processing:

1. The smell of cooking will cause saliva to form in our mouths, which is the first stage in the digestive process.

2. The sight of something dangerous approaching will trigger the stress reaction. This supplies extra energy for an escape, without waiting for it to be extracted from our food.

Near ultraviolet
There is no obvious direct link between the near ultraviolet received by our eyes and the control of the processing of food. But there may

be an indirect link, which allows our bodies to process food more effectively during the day. Possibly nocturnal animals are organised so that their digestive systems work better during the hours of darkness.

More important for us is the production of vitamin D, by the action of near ultraviolet on the skin. This is not part of the control of food digestion. It is the way nature has found to supply us with one of the vitamins essential for life.

Carbon dioxide
We breathe out carbon dioxide, which is the product of our food being oxidised.

Waste
This is what is left over after our bodies have oxidised the food, and what we excrete through the kidneys and bowels *etc.*

Meeting your requirements
The way your body digests its food can be compared to an engine burning fuel. The energy generated by an engine is obtained from the energy stored in the fuel. In the same way the energy we need for our bodies is generated by our food.

The energy in food is measured in units called calories (kilocalories in full). The average daily energy requirement for our bodies is 2500 calories. Ideally we should match the number of calories to our energy needs. This is how you would run an engine to maximise efficiency, and avoid clogging it up by burning too rich a mixture.

Calorie controlled diets make the following assumptions:

1. If you eat fewer calories than your energy needs, then you will extract the shortfall from the energy stored in body fats, which will result in weight loss.

2. If you exercise more, and don't eat any extra, the additional energy you require will be taken from the energy stores in body fats, which again will result in weight loss.

These assumptions are correct, but the following points also need considering:

- If you relax the harsh calorie counting, then you will very quickly put back the weight you have just managed to lose.

- Our digestive system is not just an energy producer like an engine. It is also extracting material for building and maintenance, so there is a lot more going on than just straightforward oxidisation. Calorie counting is useful, but results are sometimes disappointing.

- There is a multimillion pound industry that thrives on the concept of calorie controlled diets. To market their low calorie foods they need to convince people that calorie controlled diets always work.

To manage your physical well-being effectively, including getting your weight down to what it should be, we need to look further than just counting calories.

Taking exercise
Exercise is an important contributor towards health and well-being.

Boosting metabolism
Your metabolic, or oxidation rate, is a measure of how efficiently you burn up your food. Taking regular exercise, even in modest amounts, improves your metabolic rate, without increasing your appetite.

Doing aerobics
Aerobic exercise supplies oxygen to our muscles. All steady, continuous exercises are aerobic, for example: walking, cycling and swimming.
  Aerobic exercise is the best form of exercise, because it replaces fatty muscle with lean muscle. This is good for long-term weight loss.

Helping your heart
Taking regular exercise decreases blood pressure, and improves the health of your heart and lungs.

Finding ways to take exercise
Just 15 minutes of aerobic exercise each day counts as regular exercise. Daily exercise is better than doing the same total once or twice a week, but daily exercise isn't always practical.
  Here are some suggestions for increasing your exercise:

- Try walking part of the way to work. You can park your car a mile away and walk the last bit, or get off the bus a stop early.

- Walk your children to school, instead of taking them by car and then walk back home briskly. But try to avoid walking near busy roads, where the air is likely to be polluted.

- If you go away a lot on business, always choose a hotel with a pool and have a good swim before dinner.

- Try to find 15 minutes in the day to follow one of the many aerobics videos available on the market.

- Go for long cycle rides at the weekend. Country parks are better than roads to avoid taking in a lot of polluted air.

- If you work in an office building, walk up and down the stairs, rather than using the lift.

- Organisers of courses and seminars should set aside time to allow the delegates to go for a 15 minute walk each day.

Shopping for your needs

Let us look at the food we eat in more detail. Food can be divided under three main headings: fat, carbohydrates and protein. Scientists believe that our bodies are designed to take in these foods in the following proportions: fat 18 per cent, carbohydrate 65 per cent, protein 17 per cent. This is known as the caveman diet, because it is what our early ancestors would have eaten.

Here is a brief summary of what type of food falls into each of the three categories. Some things appear under more than one heading. Eggs for example are a good source of protein, but they also contain fat.

Fat
Meat, cheese, eggs, butter, margarine.

Carbohydrates
Grains, potatoes, vegetables, rice, fruit. Fibre is also an important carbohydrate. You don't get any energy from fibre, but it is necessary to include fibre in your diet so that your digestive system works properly.

Protein
Eggs, rice, beans, nuts, dairy products, meat.

Making Hay

In the 1920s a Dr Hay suggested that certain combinations of foods should be avoided. For example, you should not eat protein, such as meat, at the same time as a carbohydrate, like potatoes. This was based on his belief that our digestive system can only cope effectively with one type of food at a time.

Those who are interested in learning more about the Hay's diet, known as the **Food Combining Diet**, will find there are still plenty of books being written about it. As an idea it has never really gone out of fashion. And there are some similarities with the Hay's diet, and the ideas that have come from metabolic typing.

Swallowing a difficult idea

Dr Kelley, who developed the concept of metabolic typing, also came up with a list of foods to suit the two main bio-types. The reasoning behind the choices is difficult to follow, but the basic concept boils down to:

1. You can become much less able to digest some types of food.

2. You can develop a requirement for more of certain vitamins and minerals, and this can lead to your becoming deficient in these.

3. Your intolerances and needs are related to your bio-type, so different people need to eat different things.

Causes could be due to:

- changes as you get older
- being in an out-of-balance situation resulting from an excess or deficiency
- a combination of both.

An example will demonstrate why these ideas are important. Imagine that your digestive system has become less able to burn up the fat in your food. Your body will now take more from the carbohydrate, which it is still able to burn efficiently. The fat that is not consumed will stay in your body, and you will put on weight. Unfortunately this means all fat – even low fat spreads. This explains why calorie controlled diets do not always work. The *type* of food you eat needs to be taken into consideration, not just how many calories it contains.

Figure 26 lists the foods suited to each of the two bio-types. Vitamins and minerals have been included. We will be looking at these in detail later in this chapter. You can then use the information from the food list to help you draw up your own personal action plan for achieving well-being.

	Left-biased (Fast metabolism)	Right-biased (Slow metabolism)
You will be tolerant of:	Red meat Dairy products Root vegetables Corn products Barley products Beer and whisky	Eggs Fish Poultry Leafy green vegetables Fruit and wine

You may need extra:	*Vitamins*: A, B_{12}, C
	   and E
	Minerals: Calcium
	   and Zinc
		Vitamins: B_1, B_2, B_3,
		   B_6 and D
		Minerals:
		Magnesium and
		Potassium

You will probably have become intolerant to:	Leafy green vegetables Fruit and wine Wheat products	Red meat Oils and fats Dairy products

Fig. 26. Foods that suit the two bio-types.

Matching your metabolism

Fast metabolism
The main advantage of having a fast metabolism is that you are reasonably tolerant of fatty foods. However, you are likely to be intolerant of green vegetables (*eg* sprouts), fruit (particularly citrus) and wine. You should avoid supplementing your diet with the normal variety of vitamin C, as this is too acidic. A *buffered* vitamin C is available as an alternative.

Slow metabolism
People with a slow metabolism are ideally suited to the traditional

healthy diet of green vegetables and fresh fruit. Slow metabolism means that you have a poor digestion for a wide range of fatty and fried foods, so you should avoid red meat and fast food outlets. You should also be aware of the dangers of hydrogenated oils used in manufactured foods, which include: margarine, cakes and chocolate. Spreads made from non-hydrogenated oils are available in health food stories. Dairy products, such as milk, butter and cheese, are also likely to cause you both physical and emotional problems. You should therefore aim to have as little of these as possible in your diet.

FENDING OFF EXCESSES

We will now look at the things you don't need – excesses – and how these result in getting out of balance. Remember that an excess will try to push you round the unbalance and recovery cycle, illustrated in Figure 2.

Betting on the odds

People tend to defend bad habits with such statements as: 'I could just as easily be run over by a bus as die from smoking 20 cigarettes a day.' This argument introduces a possible cause of death – the bus – which applies to non-smokers as well as smokers. This appears to equalise the risk.

However, the mathematics of risk doesn't work this way. A smoker risks being hit by a bus, *and* risks dying through a smoking-related disease. This means there is a higher total risk to a smoker than a non-smoker.

We do not have a built-in mechanism which stops us physically abusing ourselves through what we eat, drink or inhale. It is up to each individual to manage his or her own physical well-being. Cutting down, or preferably cutting out, any undesirable excesses is the only way to reduce the risk of physical or emotional damage.

Kicking the habit

Some of the things that you take in excess of your normal requirements can lead to addiction, such as coffee and alcohol. Addiction means being dependent on the stimulating effects the substance provides. The following pattern occurs:

1. With regular use you damage your endocrine nervous system.

2. Now you need to take more of the substance to produce the same stimulating effect.

3. If you try to stop, you not only miss the feeling of stimulation, you experience withdrawal symptoms, which can be quite unpleasant. So you carry on taking it, unable to kick the habit, and continue to cause more damage to your body.

Suffering from an allergy

Sometimes you can experience an allergic reaction to a substance that is eaten, breathed in, or touched. This happens when the substance causes your immune system to retaliate unnecessarily.

In theory the immune system should only attack what is likely to harm you, but sometimes it doesn't work properly. The allergic reaction is not necessarily linked to the substance itself. The immune system is making a mistake because it has been damaged, and this damage may have resulted from something completely different.

Note

It is possible to be allergic to one or more of the goods that suit your bio-type, as detailed in Figure 26. For example, a person with fast metabolism might be allergic to cows milk. Allergy is different from intolerance, most notably in the time it takes for the effects to be noticed. An allergic reactions happens almost right away, but it can be many hours before an intolerance takes effect. Allergies can be identified by a process of elimination, or a food allergy test. (See the Useful Addresses section for more information about tests.)

CUTTING OUT EXCESSES

Let us examine each of the excesses that can have a detrimental effect on our well-being.

Suffering from stress

Stress is part of our natural defence against danger. The stress reaction is there to get you out of danger fast, or to give you extra strength to fight an enemy. But it can be damaging if you don't use up the extra energy supplied.

Unnecessary stress will:

• Cause your body to age by slowing down cell repair.

- Interfere with your digestion, which can in some cases lead to a weight increase.

- Become addictive if prolonged, because you begin to need more stress to produce the same stimulating effect.

Stress can be the result of a number of different problems. And the action you need to take depends on the root cause. Appropriate action is summarised below.

Pressure or pace of life
Stress can result from too much work, or a serious illness in the family. See the Further Reading section for suggested books on stress management.

Difficulties with a personal relationship
Use each other's personality profiles to identify clashes of personality.

- Try to appreciate that each person is different.

- Discuss problems.

- Accept people for who they are. Don't feel you can change them – their blueprint is firmly embedded in their nervous system.

Being unhappy at work
What *you* are like may not fit in with current management style:

- Try to steer clear of situations you are uncomfortable with, *eg* making presentations.

- Don't be afraid to say 'No'.

- Develop the things you are good at when these are relevant to the situation, *eg* having a really tidy workplace.

Taking drugs
When we talk about drugs and health, people usually think about illegal substances. But medically prescribed drugs, such as aspirin and sleeping tablets, can often be just as damaging to your well-being.

- Most drugs are addictive.

- Drugs can stimulate feelings of well-being, but this is at the cost of pushing you round the unbalance/recovery cycle (see Figure 2). Continued use will inevitably lead to illness and possibly early death.

- As with any other excess, you have no clues as to how strong your nervous system is in relation to drugs.

Taking action on drugs
- Medically prescribed drugs, such as sleeping tablets, are taken to address a symptom. However, it is always better to attack the root cause. Insomnia, for example, is often the result of stress.

- Users of illegal drugs who want help with their addiction should phone one of the help lines advertised in libraries, surgeries and other public buildings.

Smoking tobacco
Tobacco contains the highly addictive drug, nicotine.

- The tobacco companies rely on people's addiction to nicotine, to maintain their profits.

- People give a number of reasons for why they continue to smoke – but there really is only one: addiction.

- Nicotine addiction is very harmful by itself, but tobacco also contains other dangerous chemicals. This cocktail of excesses is likely to lead you down the path to:
  - premature aging
  - bronchial problems
  - circulation problems
  - heart disease
  - loss of sex drive
  - premature death from lung cancer.

Taking action on smoking
Nicotine addiction is powerful and hard to break. Often it can take a serious threat to health before a smoker acts. For many people this comes too late.

- Be honest with yourself and try to see what smoking is doing to your well-being. Study the unbalance and recovery cycle in Figure 2.

- Make giving up smoking part of your personal action plan for well-being.

- Enlist the help of a close friend to bully you into giving it up, and then to monitor your progress.

Drinking alcohol

Too much alcohol can lead to alcoholism, which is an addiction. Alcohol is not essential for human life, but the following points need considering:

- There is a view that a small amount of alcohol is beneficial for improving blood circulation.

- Alcohol has been around for thousands of years. In many societies it is a catalyst for interaction between people.

- Socialising over drinks probably helps to reduce stress.

Taking action on alcohol
- Always drink in moderation.

- Never drink alone, to drown your sorrows.

- Confine drinking to social occasions, preferably in relaxed situations.

- Stay within the drinking and driving limits.

Consuming coffee

Coffee can be just as damaging to your health as any of the other excesses.

- Coffee is a complex substance, distantly related to narcotic drugs.

- Coffee is a stimulant that sets off the stress reaction, so it can lead to excessive stress.

- You can become addicted to coffee. The withdrawal symptoms are headaches and a lack of energy.

- Typical effects of too much coffee are:
  - restlessness
  - nervousness
  - flushed face
  - insomnia
  - rapid pulse and palpitations
  - digestion problems.

- Decaffeinated coffee has no real advantage over ordinary coffee. It still contains chemicals that have been linked to:
  - cancer
  - the body being drained of essential minerals.

Taking action on coffee
- Try to cut down your coffee drinking, or stop altogether. Tea and cola drinks also contain caffeine, so be careful not to overdo these either.

- If you are running meetings at work, or training courses, always ensure there is an adequate supply of alternative drinks for those who are trying to avoid coffee.

- If you do have problems with coffee, then you may also need to avoid food containing nuts and chocolate, as these are all related.

Sweetening with sugar
Our bodies are not designed to consume simple carbohydrates in the form of sugar.

- The body over-reacts to increased blood sugar levels, reducing them sharply. Symptoms are:
  - difficulty in concentrating
  - forgetfulness
  - blank mind.

- Sugar slows up the process by which calcium gets from your blood into your bones. This can be a contributory factor in osteoarthritis.

- Children with high sugar levels in their diets can suffer from:
  - aggressive behaviour
  - nervousness
  - depression
  - inability to concentrate
  - insomnia
  - headaches
  - digestive problems
  - allergies.

  All of these symptoms can be relieved by taking more sugar – so this can be classed as an addiction.

- We have got into the habit of swilling down our food with sweet drinks, like canned colas. Our digestive process starts in the mouth with the production of saliva. We don't need to drink with food.

Taking action on sugar

- Cut down on or cut out foods containing refined sugar – you will gradually lose your sweet tooth.

- Don't overdo honey and concentrated fruit drinks that contain natural sugar.

- Always read the labels on food to look for hidden sugar.

- Reduce and then try to eliminate sugar on breakfast cereals and in tea.

- Discourage children from developing a sweet tooth. Sweets, chocolate, biscuits, and drinks provide an excess of sugar.

Sprinkling on salt

Salt is the chemical sodium chloride. Sodium is a mineral that we need very little of for normal body functions. Humans have got into the habit of using a lot of salt and developed a taste for it.

- Recommended intake is around 3mgs per day, but the average intake per person is 12 mgs per day.

- Salt raises blood pressure, which can lead to heart problems.

- Salt places an extra burden on the kidneys, while they are trying to do their best to clear out other harmful things from your body.

- Salt is added to fast foods, potato crisps, *etc*, to enhance the flavour, and possibly to induce a thirst to persuade you to buy more drink. Potato crisps contain a lot of fat. So they are not a good thing to feed to children.

Taking action on salt
- If you have a persistent urge to take salt, this may be due to a zinc deficiency (see information about zinc on page 106).

- Avoid eating fast foods and crisps known to contain a lot of salt.

- Don't add salt to flavour your cooking – try using herbs instead.

- Don't add salt to your food at the table.

- Apply these guidelines to all members of your family, especially your children.

Reducing fat
The caveman diet suggests that our bodies are designed to cope with food containing only 18 per cent fat. Modern diets, however, contain around 40 per cent fat, and people who frequent chip shops and fast food outlets may have an even higher fat intake than this.

- Saturated fats that come from red meat are more damaging than unsaturated vegetable fats and oils from fish.

- There can be a lot of hidden fat in processed foods, such as fast food. The fat is put there to make you feel satisfied after eating.

- Excessive amounts of saturated fat can lead to:
  – strokes
  – heart attacks
  – breast cancer
  – diabetes
  – gallstones
  – acne
  – obesity.

Taking action on fat
Steer clear of foods containing hidden fat, such as fast foods, and

potato crisps. If it's got a label, always check it before eating.

- Everyone will benefit from cutting down on foods containing saturated fat; these include:
  - red meat
  - eggs
  - butter
  - cheese
  - milk
  - margarine.

- Suggested alternatives to red meat are:
  - fish
  - poultry.

- People with right-biased nervous systems are particularly vulnerable to putting on weight as a result of consuming fat – even in relatively small amounts. (See Figure 26.)

Avoiding pollution

Air pollution has direct access to our nervous system, through our lungs and bloodstream. The main trouble-makers are oxides, and one of these is **ozone**. In the upper atmosphere, ozone is a highly desirable filter, which prevents us receiving harmful UV-C. But at ground level, ozone is positively dangerous to human well-being.

- Oxides, like ozone, are produced by vehicle exhaust fumes – made worse by the action of sunlight.

- The scientific name given to these oxides is **free radicals**, and they are aggressive chemicals that roam about with nowhere to go.

- The body naturally tries to fight the presence of oxides. But to work properly it needs a plentiful supply of vitamins A, C and E, plus the mineral **selenium**. This combination is known as an antioxidant.

Taking action of pollution
- Avoid walking, cycling or jogging along roads with heavy traffic, particularly on still, warm summer days.

- If you are relocating your company, try to minimise the use of cars by your employees, by locating where good public transport already exists. We need to reverse the trend of locating companies in greenfield sites along motorway corridors.

• At weekends go for walks in the country or by the sea, rather than going out for a drive in the car.

• Planners should always consider the people who live in an area, and the effects of pollution, when they are designing road traffic schemes.

• Take a daily dose of the vitamins A, C and E plus selenium.

Taking care with toxins
Toxic substances can get into our bodies through food and drink. The main toxins, their possible effects, and how to avoid them are summarised in Figure 27.

Shielding yourself against radiation
We are being bombarded by electromagnetic radiation, which comes from daylight, gamma rays and radio waves.

Daylight – visible light, near ultraviolet and infra-red (heat) occurs naturally, originating from the sun. All other radiation from the sun is filtered out by the upper atmosphere.

Gamma rays – from naturally occurring background nuclear decay. In some places in the UK, gamma rays come from radon gas, which is only a problem if it gets trapped inside buildings.

Radio waves – are entirely man-made, apart from the occasional lightning discharge. The radio spectrum is filled from end to end – from the longest wavelengths, down to micro-wavelengths.

Radio waves are harmless when you are remote from transmitting aerials. They are used in microwave ovens. Food is cooked because micro-wavelength signals induce electric currents inside the food.

There is some doubt about the safety of mobile phones because the transmitting aerial is right next to your head. The power output is very low, but everyone has a different tolerance level to excesses, and some people may be vulnerable even to these low powers.

There is also a question mark over very long wave radiation, from high voltage power lines and railway overhead cables. The long lines may act as aerials, and some people may be vulnerable even to low powers generated.

Toxin	Sources	What it does	How to avoid it
Lead	Car exhaust fumes	Children are most at risk, but adults can suffer too Symptoms include: aggressive behaviour, disturbed sleep, and headaches	Apply advice on air pollution in previous section. Vitamin C in the diet helps combat the effects of lead – also calcium and zinc
	Old water pipes		Run taps for a while each morning, to flush out the standing water
Aluminium	Cooking utensils Food wrapping	Linked to senile dementia	Avoid using aluminium pots and kettles, and if possible foil wrapping foods during cooking
Additives & preservatives	These have E numbers and are added to food to enhance colour and to give it a longer life	Behavioural problems in children such as hyperactivity	Go for fresh food and drink
Pesticides	Sprayed on fruit, cereals and vegetables Gets into meat through animal feeds	Illness and poisoning	Buy organic produce. Grow your own fruit and vegetables. Farmers need to take care with amounts of chemicals used

Fig. 27. Summary table of toxins.

Taking action on mobile phones
- Avoid long periods of use against your head.

- Never place the phone aerial in your mouth, or near your eyes.

- The preferred method is to use your phone with a car kit and external aerial.

- Think about the well-being of others when you are using your phone with a car kit – don't transmit alongside crowded pavements.

Taking action on power lines
- Housing developments should be kept well clear of high voltage power lines, substations, and railway lines with overhead cables.

- Before buying a house, thoroughly investigate the surrounding area for high voltage electric supply cables and installations, including underground high voltage routes.

- Until there is a definite conclusion to the debate about electromagnetic radiation from power lines, play safe and keep clear.

ELIMINATING DEFICIENCIES

In addition to extracting energy, your body also makes use of the vitamins and minerals in your food. Vitamins and minerals are required for:

(a) **Building** – for example, keeping your bones and teeth healthy.

(b) **Maintenance** – for example, keeping your nervous system in good order, to enable it to fight disease.

Living with a shortage
Minerals are just as important as vitamins.

> **A deficiency of a vitamin, and/or a mineral, can result in an impairment of normal body processes, illness, or even death.**

A vitamin and/or mineral deficiency will push you around the unbalance and recovery cycle (see Figure 2).

• You will only become aware of a deficiency when you get to the exhaustion stage of the unbalance and recovery cycle.

• The effects of a deficiency can be just as serious as those brought on by an excess.

• It is possible to cause a deficiency by an excess. For example, too much alcohol is likely to lead to a deficiency of the essential mineral, zinc. This means you are getting hit by an excess and a deficiency at the same time.

Dealing with deficiency

Your diet may be deficient in vitamins and/or minerals for the following reasons:

1. Depletion from food because of modern production methods.

2. Cereals and vegetables take up minerals from the soil – but modern farming methods have reduced the mineral availability.

3. You require vitamins and minerals in greater quantities as you get older, and because of specific bio-type needs.

4. Vitamins and minerals may be absent from the range of food you eat, because you are on a specialist diet, *eg* vegetarian.

Recommendation
It is better to identify and deal with vitamin and mineral deficiencies before the effects are noticed. This will avoid unnecessary damage to your body and mind.

Supplementing your diet

To address a vitamin and/or mineral deficiency, you can take the following action:

(a) Adjust your diet to increase the intake of food containing the deficient item, or

(b) Take a supplement in capsule or tablet form.

Questions and answers

Labels on food packaging show they contain plenty of vitamins. So why is it necessary to take a supplement?

Packaged foods can't be relied on to give a full range of requirements. Modern food processing tends to refine out minerals.

I think I'd feel like a hypochondriac if I had to swallow tablets every day. Aren't people who take supplements just cranks?

After you have taken action to correct a deficiency, the improvement in well-being can be so significant that you'll never want to stop taking the supplement.

Aren't vitamin and mineral supplements expensive?

The initial purchase can be expensive. But it usually works out as the equivalent of just a few pence a day. Think of supplements as part of your regular diet, and include it in your shopping budget. And if you've given up a bad habit like smoking, or excessive drinking, you can use part of the money saved to buy your supplements.

Identifying your needs

There isn't a simple method available for you to identify individual vitamin and mineral requirements. But you can make a good estimate by examining the range of food you eat.

The following tables can be used for guidance:

- Vitamin table – see Figure 28.
- Mineral table – see Figure 29.

Here are the steps which will help you to identify your personal needs (photocopy the tables so that you don't have to mark the book):

1. Start with the vitamin table. Using a high-light pen, mark the foods you regularly eat – marking right across the rows, from left to right.

2. Look down each of the columns in turn. There should be at least one tick covered by a high-lighted line in each column. This shows that you are receiving a vitamin from your food.

3. Where you have a vitamin not covered by your normal range of

food, mark this by circling the name at the top of the column.

4. Repeat steps 1, 2 and 3 using the mineral table.

5. Draw up a list of your requirements from:
   (a) the information gathered in this exercise, and
   (b) the additional information provided by the following notes.

Notes
The following notes will help you to make a more accurate assessment of your needs.

Recommended daily allowance (RDA)
The RDA figures are at the bottom of each column in the vitamin and mineral tables. If you do need to take a supplement, then the RDA should be used as the guide to how much.

Bio-type individual requirements
Refer to Figure 26, which shows the foods that suited the two main bio-types. This indicates where additional vitamins and minerals are likely to be required, and supplements may have to be taken. Extra potassium should be obtained by eating more leafy green vegetables.

Vitamin B_6
This is toxic in high doses. It should only be taken in conjunction with other B vitamins. This is called a vitamin B complex.

Vitamin D
This is best produced by the action of sunlight on the skin of the face and hands. But in the spring you may have to supplement your reserves, if you are not eating food that naturally contains vitamin D.

Selenium
Selenium levels in UK soils are low. Most people are likely to be deficient in this mineral, unless eating a lot of fish or brazil nuts. You are recommended to take a supplement of selenium together with vitamins A, C and E. This combination acts as an antioxidant, to help combat the effects of air pollution. Selenium is also thought to offer protection against several forms of cancer, including breast cancer.

Chromium
A high intake of refined sugar and flour, which is a feature of the

	A	B$_1$ Thiamin	B$_2$ Riboflavin	B$_3$ Niacin	B$_5$ Pantothenic Acid	B$_6$ Pyridoxine	B$_{12}$	Folic Acid	Biotin	C	D	E
Bananas						✓						
Beans		✓										
Blackcurrants										✓		
Breakfast cereals		✓		✓		✓						
Broccoli								✓		✓		
Brown rice		✓							✓			
Brussel sprouts										✓		
Cabbage								✓				
Cheese			✓	✓			✓		✓			
Dairy products	✓											
Dried fruit					✓							
Eggs	✓		✓		✓		✓		✓		✓	✓
Fish	✓			✓		✓	✓				✓	
Fruit	✓											
Green leafy vegetables			✓									✓
Green peppers										✓		
Kiwi fruit										✓		
Liver	✓				✓	✓		✓			✓	
Meat				✓			✓		✓			
Milk			✓	✓			✓					
Nuts					✓			✓				
Oranges										✓		
Peanuts												✓
Peas		✓								✓		
Potatoes				✓						✓		
Poultry				✓		✓						
Pulses					✓			✓				
Vegetables	✓											
Vegetable oils												✓
Wholemeal bread				✓	✓	✓			✓			✓
Yoghurt									✓			
RDA	800	1.4	1.6	18	6	2	1	200	0.15	60	5	10
	mcg	mg	mg	mg	mg	mg	mg	mcg	mg	mg	mg	mg

Fig. 28. The vitamin table.

	Calcium	Iron	Magnesium	Zinc	Potassium	Selenium	Chromium
Cereals				✓			✓
Cheese	✓			✓			✓
Dairy products	✓			✓			
Eggs		✓					
Fish						✓	✓
Fruit					✓		✓
Green leafy vegetables	✓	✓	✓	✓	✓		✓
Liver		✓					✓
Meat		✓		✓			✓
Milk	✓						
Nuts			✓			* see note	
Pasta			✓				
Peas			✓				
Seafood							
Seeds						✓	
Shellfish				✓		✓	
Soya beans			✓				
Wholemeal flour					✓	✓	✓
RDA	800mg	14mg	300mg	15mg	–	100mcg	200mcg

*Two brazil nuts will provide the RDA

Fig. 29. The mineral table.

modern diet, tends to drain this essential mineral from our bodies. Chromium assists with the digestion of fat and helps to protect against heart disease and diabetes. A supplement is recommended as a precautionary measure.

Pregnancy
Women trying to get pregnant, or who are pregnant, have special needs. They should always follow the advice given to them by their doctor or the clinic, and not attempt to work a plan out for themselves.

TAKING PERSONAL ACTION

Drawing up a personal action plan will help you to achieve physical and emotional well-being.

The personal action plan will allow you to manage changes to your lifestyle, in order to achieve specific well-being objectives.

You will be pleasantly surprised at how quickly your well-being can improve, once you start to take action. For example, adjusting for a deficiency like zinc can bring about a dramatic improvement in just a few days.

You can use the personal action plan either by yourself, or with the help of a friend or partner who acts as your mentor. If you complete a plan with another person you will be able to help and support each other.

Taking the right steps

An example of a completed plan is illustrated in Figure 30. Draw up your own plan based on this one. The steps for completing your personal action plan are as follows:

1. Fill in your name in the space at the top. This is *your* personal plan.

2. In the **where I am now** section, say what you feel is wrong.

3. In the **where I want to be** section, say what you want to achieve.

4. Then set a date by when you would like to achieve your well-being objective. The objective is all about getting from **where I am now** to **where I want to be**. Set yourself a realistic date, for example:

  - 1 month to implement a simple plan, *eg* giving up smoking.
  - 3 months to implement an average plan, like losing weight.
  - 6 months if you feel you will only be able to cope by making changes one at a time.

5. Against each of the six key points in the main section:
   - Write in what action you intend to take.
   - Base statements on the information you have gathered about yourself as you have worked through this book.
   - If no action is required in a section, then mark 'none'.
   The main sources of information about yourself are:
   1. your personal profile card – see Figure 21
   2. table of foods that suit the two bio-types, see Figure 26.

6. Against each of your action statements, write a completion date in the **by when** column.

7. Sign and date your action plan.

Monitoring progress

To help you monitor progress, a series of reviews are undertaken. You can do these reviews by yourself, or with the help of a friend, or if you are paired up with someone also doing an action plan, you can act as each other's mentors.

1. Agree review dates with your mentor.
   - Have the first review immediately after your action plan has been drawn up.
   - For short plans (one month) hold reviews weekly.
   - For longer plans, hold reviews each month.
   - Have a final review meeting just after the end date of your action plan.

2. Before meeting, mark off progress of each action in the **completed** column of the Personal Action Plan.

3. On completion of the action plan, check that you have achieved where you want to be.

4. Consider taking further action by drawing up another plan, to make further gains or improvements.

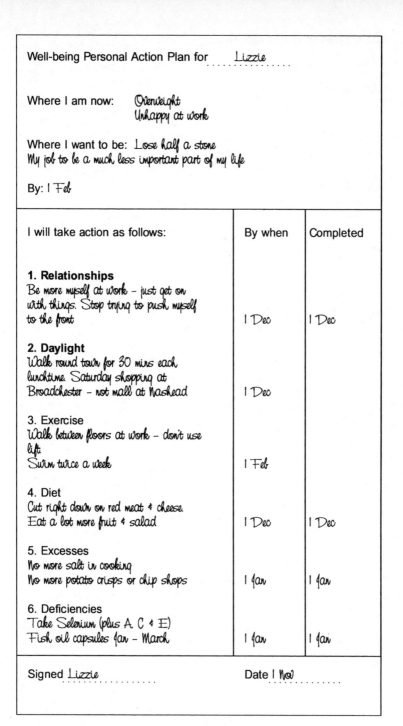

Well-being Personal Action Plan for Lizzie

Where I am now: Overweight
Unhappy at work

Where I want to be: Lose half a stone
My job to be a much less important part of my life

By: 1 Feb

I will take action as follows:	By when	Completed
1. Relationships Be more myself at work – just get on with things. Stop trying to push myself to the front	1 Dec	1 Dec
2. Daylight Walk round town for 30 mins each lunchtime. Saturday shopping at Broadchester – not mall at Washead	1 Dec	
3. Exercise Walk between floors at work – don't use lift. Swim twice a week	1 Feb	
4. Diet Cut right down on red meat & cheese. Eat a lot more fruit & salad	1 Dec	1 Dec
5. Excesses No more salt in cooking No more potato crisps or chip shops	1 Jan	1 Jan
6. Deficiencies Take Selenium (plus A, C & E) Fish oil capsules Jan – March	1 Jan	1 Jan

Signed Lizzie   **Date** 1 Nov

Fig. 30. Example of a completed personal action plan.

Getting your bio-type correct

The results of your bio-type test, described in Chapter 3, may have been inconclusive. You may still be unsure if you have a left or a right-biased nervous system. And this makes a difference to the action to be taken in your personal action plan.

You should draw up your action plan based on what you consider to be your most likely bio-type. If you have got it wrong, then you will not gain any improvement in your well-being.

Allow your action plan to run to the end date, then draw up another plan – this time assuming your nervous system has the opposite bias.

Holding the gains

After achieving your well-being objectives, you will want to maintain them, and not to slip back to how you were before. There are two key points that will help to prevent this.

1. You will feel so much better about yourself that you won't want to undo all your good work by reverting to bad habits.

2. You now have a good understanding of yourself. You will have read this book and understand the damage you can cause by allowing yourself to get out of balance.

Agree with your mentor to have a follow-up review meeting six months after the end date of your action plan. At this review, check that you have managed to hold the gains made. If you find that you are slipping back into old habits, then draw up another personal action plan right away.

Concluding the story

Your well-being personal action plan completes all the steps that you can take in the short term to regain physical and emotional well-being.

The final chapter deals with long-term objectives for improving your well-being, such as changing your living and working environment.

CHECKLIST OF KEY POINTS

Getting out of balance

1. Your body and mind can get out of balance as the result of an excess or a deficiency or both.

2. The resulting tendencies are always negative, such as putting on weight or becoming more nervous.

Counting calories

1. We process our food to give us energy, produce heat, and to build and maintain our bodies.

2. People of different bio-types process their food in different ways, and require different diets for physical and emotional well-being.

3. Calorie controlled diets restrict intake, but the results can be disappointing.

4. Aerobic exercise replaces fatty muscle with lean muscle.

5. Our basic foods needs are: fat 18 per cent, carbohydrate 65 per cent and protein 17 per cent.

6. The Hay's diet suggests we should not eat some types of food in combination.

Excesses

1. Subjecting yourself to an excess carries a risk of illness.

2. Some excesses are addictive.

3. Some excesses may lead to you developing an allergy.

4. To achieve physical and emotional well-being, you need to cut down, or preferably cut out, all excesses.

Deficiencies

1. You can be deficient in vitamins and/or minerals.

2. You will only be aware of a deficiency when you reach the exhaustion stage of the unbalance and recovery cycle.

3. A change of diet or a supplement will sort out a deficiency.

Personal action plan

1. A personal action plan can be used to help you achieve physical and emotional well-being.

2. Progress of your actions should be monitored by having regular reviews.

3. A friend can act as a mentor to help you to manage your personal action plan.

CASE STUDIES

David's marriage is back on track

We have already met David, in a case study at the end of Chapter 3. He thought his problem might be due to drinking too much coffee, so he cut his consumption right down. But although this helped, and he started to feel calmer, another more serious difficulty has arisen.

David and his wife used to have an enjoyable and healthy physical relationship. But David now finds he has lost interest in sex. As a consequence, he goes away on business trips as much as possible, which is easier than being at home and facing the emotional upsets this causes.

David's wife wonders if his problems are caused by his diet. She persuades him to check that what he is eating is right for his bio-type, and to draw up a personal action plan.

David had been trying to eat a lot of salads and vegetarian meals, in an effort to reduce his weight. He discovers, however, that he has a left-biased nervous system and that this type of diet is not suitable for his needs. He also identifies that he is probably deficient in the mineral zinc.

David adjusts his diet, and takes a zinc supplement. He loses half a stone in two months, and begins to recover his sex drive. As a result life at home is more relaxed, and his marriage is back on track.

Jessica and Paul learn to compromise

Jessica and Paul live together in a house with a large garden. Jessica has a Gemini personality and Paul is an Aquarian. Jessica has a need for emotional warmth and Paul does not like emotional demands. So when Jessica does manage to express her feelings, Paul is unable to respond appropriately. This causes difficulties in their relationship.

As time goes by, their relationship grows more and more unsteady. Jessica becomes much more edgy than she used to be, and Paul depressed and morose. Also, in spite of eating plenty of home grown fruit and vegetables that Paul produces in his garden, the couple find they are gaining weight.

They undertake a bio-typing exercise, which shows that they are opposite types. They then each draw up personal action plans.

They first of all have to learn to appreciate their personalities are different, and that the other person is not likely to change. They also find that they need to follow different diets in order to keep their weight down.

They have always loved each other, and are prepared to make the compromises necessary. They each go ahead with their action plans and adjust their diets. Soon their weight gets back to normal, and the partnership settles down again into a loving relationship.

Painful action, but Sam pulls through

Samantha is 23 years of age, and has smoked cigarettes since the age of 16.

Friends have tried to talk her into giving it up, but she has always strongly defended her right to smoke. She is, of course, addicted to nicotine.

When a close friend explains how the unbalance and recovery cycle works, Sam realises she may have already done herself a lot of harm. So she decides it is time to quit.

Sam's personal action plan is simple. She immediately stops smoking, and throws away her remaining cigarettes. She has to suffer the agony of withdrawal, but she has the support of her friend who acts as her mentor. They hold weekly review meetings to check on Sam's progress.

They agree to have a further review meeting, six months after Sam quit smoking. At this meeting, Sam reports how much better she feels. And that she has no intention of ever going back to cigarettes.

6

Building in Well-Being

INFLUENCING OUR SENSES

So far we have discussed how physical influences play an important part in our well-being. There are a wide range of physical influences, including daylight, vitamins and food type. In this chapter we will look at the effects of sensory influences – in particular the visual impact of our environment.

Sizing up sensory influences

Sensory influences can be just as important to our well-being as physical influences but they tend to be forgotten.

They are less obvious than physical influences, and affect us in more subtle ways. However, they can be just as powerful, in that they can push us around the cycle of unbalance and recovery (see Figure 2), and cause us to:

- become unwell
- become unhappy
- have difficulties with relationships
- be uncertain about our role in life.

Sensory influences often go hand in hand with physical influences. For example, someone living in a flat without a garden is likely to be deficient in natural daylight. And if the building is in a state of decay, then the sensory effects of the bad surroundings will significantly add to that person's difficulties.

Unfortunately, our surroundings are largely under the control of such professions as:

- civil engineers
- architects
- town planners
- members of parliament

so that in a sense the well-being of millions of citizens can be affected by the decisions they make.

Breaking down the barrier

Refer back to the diagram illustrated in Figure 3. The top part of the picture refers to *thinking* and the lower part to the *control* of our bodies through the nervous system.

At first sight, the controlling and thinking parts of the brain appear to be separated by a barrier. The endocrine nervous system is described as autonomic – meaning it works by itself and we cannot consciously interfere. However, there are many observed situations which point to the existence of a pathway between thinking and control. Here are some examples:

1. You spot a dangerous dog approaching – the stress reaction triggers release of hormones.

2. Yoga, massage, aromatherapy, *etc*, reduce stress and tension.

3. When you smell food – your appetite is stimulated.

4. Adopting a positive attitude can often help you get over an illness more quickly.

Enjoying stress

Sometimes we deliberately put ourselves through stress. For example we ride roller coasters because of the thrill of facing danger. Provided we only do this sort of thing infrequently, it is unlikely to cause us lasting harm.

Generally, however, we are better to do without the continuous pressure from stress. Nature intended the stress reaction to provide additional energy, to enable us to fight or take flight. To complete the stress reaction properly we need to expend this energy.

People who live in run-down high-rise flats are likely to suffer stress because of visual deprivation. So they may react by expending their extra energy through, for example:

- aggressive behaviour towards their neighbours
- vandalism and car theft.

They may also take drugs in an attempt to blot out the harshness of their surroundings.

Turning on calm

Sensory influences can be placed into three categories:

1. *Negative*: harmful because they push us into the unbalance and recovery cycle. Areas of urban decay and harsh angular buildings are a source of strong negative sensory influence.

2. *Free-wheeling*: a lack of any sensory influences, either negative or positive. Sleeping, for example, gives your mind a rest as well as your body. There are several ways of shutting out external sensory influences. Some fitness centres have flotation tanks and a session in one of these is said to be very relaxing. Another example is yoga, which requires an intense focus of the mind on the body and shuts out sensory influences. The disadvantages of these methods is that the benefits can be short-lived.

3. *Positive*: ensures the stress reaction is switched off. For example, relaxing to classical music will keep stress at bay. **Visual messages**, however, are the most powerful. This is why we get drawn to towns with character and beautiful countryside.

    The key points about positive sensory influences are as follows:

    - They are an essential human need, in order to maintain balance and ensure well-being.

    - You cannot have too much of a positive sensory influence – unlike physical influences, which must match your needs. You can overdose on a vitamin, but you will come to no harm if you spend a long time in the countryside.

    - Different people will require different amounts of positive sensory influences to ensure they maintain their individual balance points.

    - It is possible to have living and working environments with sufficient positive sensory influence to meet everyone's needs. The method of achieving this is discussed in the next section.

Harmonising nature's forces

Feng shui is the ancient Chinese art of ensuring you live in harmony with the forces of nature. The basis of feng shui is achieving the correct balance between two opposing forces called **yin** and **yang**.

This balance is identical to the **positive sensory influences** which keep our surroundings stress free. You can build more detail into your own designs for interiors and gardens by supplementing the basic principles of this chapter with the rules of feng shui.

UNLOCKING THE INFLUENCES

Let us now look in more detail at how our surroundings influence us in a sensory way. For example, people can feel unwell at work due to Sick Building Syndrome. The root cause of this may be partly, or mainly, due to the effects of sensory influences. Also, if we understand how sensory influences work, then we can make practical use of this knowledge. It is particularly helpful for interior decorating projects, and garden design.

Applying common sense

Most of what we see around us has been rearranged or put there as a result of centuries of human activity, *eg* agriculture, homes, shops, offices and industry.

In recent years there has been a significant change in the way our environment is being managed. Examples of the difference in approach are:

Traditional approach	New approach
Roads built around restrictions.	Machines cut through hills. Buildings are pulled down to clear a route.
Buildings made from local materials and to regional designs.	Manufactured materials shipped all over the world. Buildings designed on the drawing board miles from the site.

This shift has been both rapid and subtle. The traditional approach was around for thousands of years; the new approach gathered pace only after the Second World War. Many people have not noticed it has happened.

Often people feel uneasy about their living and working environment, but cannot quite put their fingers on what is wrong. Those who are aware of what has happened feel powerless to do anything about it. The unease people feel is an indicator of the existence of the detrimental effects on our well-being.

Facing up to the challenge
The way things are done now is based mainly on the principle of financial gain. The supporters of the new approach justify it by attacking the traditionalist viewpoint, and labelling everything new as modernistic and exciting – an indication of a country's wealth and power.

But supporters of the traditional approach do have a strong case. The modernists cannot demonstrate that their approach makes any positive contribution to the well-being of the population as a whole.

Sorting out the principles
The way we feel about our surroundings is directly linked to the astral and terrestrial influences which were introduced in Chapter 1. Human development has necessitated a third influence, that of functionality.

All buildings, towns, open spaces, *etc*, involve a mixture of astral, terrestrial and functional ideas. The proportion of each depends on what the building or space is to be used for.

Astral
Buildings that take into account astral influences are typically cathedrals and temples. Through these buildings humans try to reflect their ideas about humanity's place in the universe.

This is often called high architecture and Stonehenge is an early example. It is thought that Stonehenge is an alternative form of the astrological calendar.

Terrestrial
Terrestrial buildings reflect local activity, involving local people and materials – sometimes called vernacular architecture.

Functional
Building in its purest form – put there just to fulfil a basic function, and nothing more. Usually labelled as modernist.

Combining all the elements
Perhaps the traditional British red telephone box can be considered a good example of all three elements: it is shaped like a temple (astral), is made from iron and glass (terrestrial) and serves a purpose (functional).

PROVIDING THE ANSWERS

There are six key points which contribute towards providing positive sensory influences and understanding these can be very useful.

1. **Capture the spirit of the place.**
- Use local materials.
- Harmonise with surroundings.
- Reflect local culture.
- Build in regional variations.

2. **Offer protection.**
- Relate vertical shapes to human form.
- Avoid pig-pens.
- Employ non-geometric shapes.
- Introduce arches.

3. **Set the right mood.**
- Appeal to all the senses.
- Focus inwardly.

4. **Give visibility of structure.**
- Choose comfortable materials.
- Avoid deceptive finishes.
- Show how things work.

5. **Defuse straight line tension.**
- Soften hard surfaces.
- Moderate angles.
- Stagger straight sides into curves.

6. **Avoid repetition.**
- Minimise symmetry.
- Vary details.
- Deviate from plans.

These key points contribute to well-being and should be born in mind when:

- designing buildings, housing developments, town plans, *etc*, which protect the well-being of the inhabitants

- undertaking decorating projects and garden designs – so that you create stress-free environments

- assessing existing buildings and places – see how they might be improved, in order to help the people who live or work there

- designing or refurbishing a business, for example a city centre café – so that it will attract more customers.

Visiting positive places

The best test for the presence of positive sensory influences is: your own intangible feeling of *just wanting to be there.*

Often when people get drawn to places, they are not sure why – they just feel a *need* to be there.

To help clarify some of the key points a case study cottage is illustrated in Figures 31 and 32.

Exercise

Take a photocopy of the sensory influences key points. Take the copy with you the next time you visit your favourite café, restaurant or pub. It will be interesting to find out whether your gut feelings about the place are backed up by the key points.

The six key points work equally well with rooms, buildings, houses, gardens, the spaces between buildings, villages, towns, cities and can be applied anywhere in the terrestrial environment.

The sort of things to look for are:

- The use of local materials, like slate or thatched roofs.

- Doorways, arches and passages that you feel invite you to walk through.

- Natural sounds and smells, like running water and pot pourri.

- Imperfections which make obvious the hand of the builder, like chisel marks on stonework.

- Areas like rooms or town squares which are not geometrically perfect.

- The detail in things – for example, shop signs and windows – which vary slightly from one building to the next.

Fig. 31. The case study cottage – front view.

Capturing the spirit of a place

Capturing the spirit of a place means that whatever you add to a place should look as though it has always been there.

Use local materials
For our case study cottage examples of different options are:

- Face the walls with flint in a chalk area.

- Build it from bricks made from local clay.

- Roof it with slate from a nearby quarry.

Avoid importing materials from another area, unless there is no suitable material available locally. If in doubt about what local materials are available, ask someone who has lived there for most of their lives.

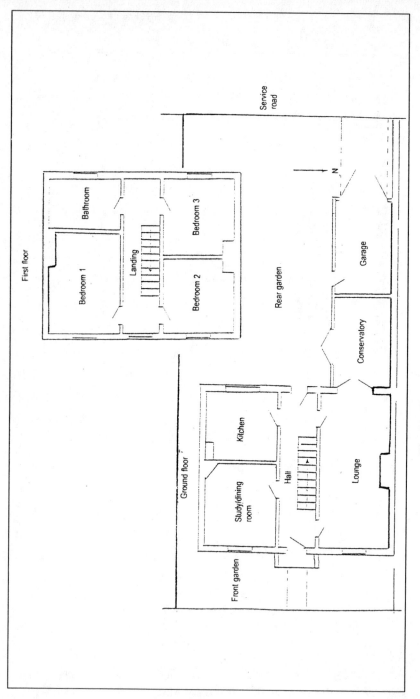

Fig. 32. The case study cottage – plans.

Harmonise with surroundings
Try to match your building or interior with what is already there.
For example:

- If extending an old farmhouse, use second-hand handmade bricks.

- If building in a woodland area, allow ivy to grow on buildings.

Avoid levelling a site and cutting down established trees to make it easier to build on.

Reflect local culture
Consider current or previous local activities. For example:

- If designing a hotel lounge in a town famous for clock making, include several working examples of locally made clocks.

- If building a small housing estate on the site of a former pottery, display house numbers on tiles, decorated with patterns from the former pottery.

Avoid importing ideas from distant places, for example, naming streets after famous people who have no connection with the area.

Building in regional variations
Counties, towns and villages often have long-standing traditional building features. These can include:

- pitch of roof

- decoration – ridge tiles, chimney pots, *etc*

- style of windows – in the case study cottage, the upstairs windows could be extended upwards to make dormer windows set into the roof.

Avoid transplanting regional variations, for example, taking English-style housing estates up to Scotland.

Offer protection
People are much more comfortable if they feel they are being

protected, rather than imprisoned by rooms and buildings.

Relate vertical shapes to human form
There are two vertical shapes people relate to:

1. *The door shape* – a rectangle which looks the right shape to walk through.

2. *The square* – which looks the right shape to walk through, with your arms outstretched on each side.

Examples of these shapes in practice include:

• rectangular and square windows – both are used in the case study cottage.

• subdivision of windows into smaller panes

• garden arches.

Avoid horizontal, picture-style windows, unless there is a need for a strong relationship with what lies outside (this point is covered later).

If you are renewing picture-style windows in your house, you might like to consider replacements with mullions, to divide the window into vertical rectangles.

Avoid pig-pens
Rectangular shapes that enclose us make us feel packaged and imprisoned. Modern offices with lots of personal computers tend to be laid out with desks grouped into pig-pen shaped areas; this uniformity usually spreads through the whole building on every floor.

Sick Building Syndrome causes employees to feel unwell for no apparent reason. One fact may be having to work long hours in artificial light. Another contributor may be the result of stress caused by working in pig-pen layouts.

It is difficult to break up this rigidity completely, because of having to run cables to the computers. However, the following ideas can be applied to reduce the overall uniformity:

• Within each pig-pen, add a plant stand, a coffee table, or sculpture.
• Stagger positions of pig-pens, to form curving passageways.

- Change floor levels, so that some pig-pens are higher than the connecting floor areas, and some are lower – but don't forget to provide wheelchair access.

- Allow employees the freedom to decorate their own spaces however they want them.

Avoid repeating the same floor layout on other floors. Vary the colour schemes too.

Employ non-geometric shapes
For new building work, squares and rectangles should be avoided. The traditional town square was never exactly square.
The following are some examples of how to employ non-geometric shapes.

- *Lounges and other rooms.* Chimney breasts and furniture help to break up the rigidity of a plain rectangular room. The case study cottage has a corner fireplace in the study.

- *Gardens.* Use plenty of trees and shrubs. Borders need curved edges.

- *Play areas.* Round off corners with planted areas.

- *Town squares and open spaces.* Allow buildings to extend beyond rigid building lines. Viewed from the air, the space should look untidy around the edges.

Avoid 'hot desks'. This is the practice in offices where employees do not have a desk of their own. They use the first desk available when they come in. People are not usually permitted to decorate desks or work areas. Decoration with personal effects breaks up rigid rectangular shapes.

Introduce arches
Arches and porches create a feeling of progression as you walk through them, particularly if they are combined with other features – typically changes in direction.
Here are some of the places where porches and arches can be used:

- As entry points to the groups of desks in the pig-pen office layout (see discussion above). These can be made from garden trellis.

- Passages between buildings in city centres can be turned into arcades by roofing them over.
  Avoid creating 'tunnels' with smooth walls and roofs.

Setting the right mood
The mood of an interior or exterior space should match its purpose.

Appealing to all the senses
Although we are mostly influenced through vision, the other senses can play their part too:

- *Touch.* Use natural materials for handrails, table tops, *etc*, and do not smother with artificial coatings, such as polyurethane varnish.

- *Smell.* Polished wood is more appealing than the artificial smell from plastic materials. Books have a distinctive smell and are nice to handle. Computer stored information is extremely useful, but books still have an important role to play in our lives.

- *Hearing.* Unwelcome noise can be very stressful. But natural sounds, like running water and birds, add to the visual sensory experience of parks and gardens.

- *Taste.* The pleasures of food and drink can be enhanced by the mood of a room. Bacon and eggs taste wonderful in a transport café, but are much less appealing in a Paris restaurant.

Avoid plastic window ledges that come with plastic framed double glazing. Use wood, preferably stripped, lightly varnished and then polished.

Focus inwardly
Setting the mood of a room can be made more difficult if outside influences are allowed to interfere. The size of windows is very important. We need to balance the view to the outside, with the amount of light required.

Sometimes the view will be included as part of the mood of the room, for example a fine view across the open sea. But sometimes we need to restrict external influences. Here are ways this can be done:

- Plant trees close to the building, so that the light through the windows is filtered by the foliage.

- Have more than one window in each room. In the case study cottage, small windows could be added to the side walls. Having two sources of light gives a higher quality of light than having a single large window.

- An open fire creates light and warmth. Coal effect gas fires are a suitable alternative to open coal or wood fires.

Avoid windowless rooms and views into building wells. People do not feel comfortable with a 100 per cent inward focus.

Giving visibility of structure
We like to pull apart what we see, seeming to take comfort in knowing how it was put together, or how it works.

Choosing comfortable materials
We are more comfortable with materials with a visible texture, or produced on a small scale, which inform us of their origin. Highly machined and artificial materials are unlikely to make a positive contribution to our feelings of well-being.
Here are some examples:

Positive	Negative
wood	steel
brick	concrete
stone	plastic
leather	nylon
small panes of glass	large panes of glass

Avoid plastic interior and exterior doors. Plastic window frames are acceptable because the material is not extensive in area, and it usually has little direct contact with people.

Avoiding deceptive finishes
Avoid trying to make unnatural materials look natural. The following examples are typical:

- Plastic cladding made to look like timber boarding.

- Plastic glazing bars in windows, to divide up large double glazed windows, placed between the two sheets of glass.

- Wooden window frames stained to look like hardwood.

Avoid the use of tropical hardwood for doors and windows because of the damage this does to the environment. Softwood will last for many years if it is suitably treated and maintained with routine painting.

Seeing how things work
We like to see how things work, rather than have the operation hidden from view. Here are some examples which have been categorised as providing a positive or negative contribution:

Positive	Negative
A pair of hinged garage doors	Up-and-over garage doors
French doors from lounge to conservatory	Sliding patio doors
Stone-built arched bridge	Motorway bridge built from reinforced concrete

Avoid poor imitations of antique devices, such as telephones with press buttons in the shape of a dial that does not turn.

Defuse straight-line tension
People do not walk in straight lines, and they do not make sudden 90 degree changes in direction. Therefore, we are not comfortable with straight lines and sharp angles.

Soften hard surfaces
We have got into the habit of expecting interior walls and ceilings to have ultra smooth finishes. These can be softened up with:

- wallpaper

- curtains at windows

- pictures and other wall decorations

- ceramic tiles in kitchens and bathrooms

- careful direction of lighting – for ceilings (shade light sources so that direct light does not reach the ceiling)

- install traditional ceiling beams in suitable rooms (works best in small rooms, for example, kitchen and dining room).

Avoid trying to texture walls and ceilings artificially with textured paint. It not only looks false, but it is very difficult to remove if you change your mind.

Moderate angles
Where walls and ceiling meet, the sharp angle should be softened. This can be done by:

- using coving

- sloping part of the ceiling. In the case study cottage, the upstairs rooms are partly under the slope of the roof. The ceiling and walls meet at an angle along two sides of the room.

Avoid using polystyrene coving. Plaster coving is available from most DIY outlets and builder's merchants.

Stagger straight sides into curves
The most pleasing curves are made up of a series of staggered straight sides (to visualise this, think about a long railway train going round a sharp bend). This principle can be applied to, for example, a group of desks in an office.
Avoid arches and other curves used, for example, over windows that are parts of circles. Pure circles are as uncomfortable to live with as rectangles.

Avoiding repetition
Modern buildings like office blocks and flats often appear stark and brutal, because of the precise repetition of windows, balconies, *etc.*

Minimise symmetry
The symmetrical designs of spaces and buildings is the first step towards having too much repetition. Here are some examples of what can be done to minimise symmetry:

- In the case study cottage change one of the downstairs windows to a small bow window.

● In a balanced garden design – disrupt the symmetry slightly, by careful choice of plants.

  Avoid using dominant items as an excuse to minimise symmetry. Garages at the front of houses both dominate and unbalance their appearance. For the case study cottage, the garage has been tucked away round the back. This also has the advantage of creating traffic-free streets in front of the houses.

Varying details
Houses and other buildings grouped together should be similar, but not the same. Here are some examples of how this can be achieved:

● An estate of case study cottages should have some houses linked together.

● Door furniture, *eg* numbers, catches, locks, *etc*, should be varied amongst a group of houses.

● Build each house a slightly different size.

Deviate from plans
Some deviation from plans should be permitted as work progresses. For example:

● When decorating an office, allow the people who are to work there to ask for alterations while work is in progress.

● During house building discuss possible changes with the client.

  Avoid being too radical. What is required is to ensure subtle differences between one room and the next, one working area and the next, or one house and the next.

CHECKLIST OF KEY POINTS

Sensory influences
1. Sensory influences can be as important to our well-being as physical influences.

2. They can push us around the cycle of unbalance and recovery.

3. Their control is largely in the hands of others, for example: town planners.

4. Negative sensory influences affect our well-being through the stress reaction.

5. Positive sensory influences ensure the stress reaction is switched off.

Sensory influences and the environment

1. The way we manage our environment has changed significantly since the Second World War.

2. Buildings, towns, open spaces, *etc*, consist of a mixture of astral, terrestrial and functional features.

3. Buildings with astral features are typically cathedrals; with terrestrial features are typically cottages; with functional features are typically multi-storey car parks.

Contributors to well-being – key points

1. Buildings, rooms and spaces can contribute to people's well-being through positive sensory influences.

2. There are six key contributors:
   - Capture the spirit of the place.
   - Offer protection.
   - Set the right mood.
   - Give visibility of structure.
   - Defuse straight line tension.
   - Reduce repetition.

3. These key points can be used to help design places that protect the well-being of the inhabitants.

4. The best test for the presence of positive sensory influence is your own feeling of wanting to be there.

CASE STUDIES

Letters mean more to Mike than rave reviews

We have already introduced Mike, in one of the case studies at the end of Chapter 1. Mike is an interior designer. He has already changed his approach to design by working more intuitively, and relying less on his computer.

Mike wants to be an even better designer, so he studies the key points which contribute to positive sensory influences. This gives him a clear understanding of the direction his designs have to take. And after several of his new ideas are put into practice, he begins to receive letters of praise from residents and office workers.

These letters mean more to Mike than any of the previous good reviews of his work in design magazines. The only people who are qualified to judge his designs are the people who live and work there.

Notorious estate rids itself of crime

The Havelock housing estate is run down and plagued by crime. But the fabric of the houses is basically sound, so the local authority feels it is worth refurbishing them.

The windows are replaced with double glazed units – a design divided into vertical rectangles, and some of the houses are given bow windows as an alternative. New wooden front doors are provided, of varying styles. The monotonous brick faces of most of the houses are rendered over with a rough plaster, then painted. The remaining houses are pebble-dashed using stones from the local gravel pit. The wide streets are narrowed, with curves introduced by extending the grass verges and a large number of deciduous trees are planted all over the estate.

While the work is making process, the residents are invited to give their views. The builders willingly make several minor adjustments to meet specific requests.

Soon after the work is finished, the crime rate falls dramatically, and it is not long before there is a waiting list of people wanting to live there.

Old building suits Sam's people very well

Leocom, a company specialising in business mobile communications, is moving to new premises. The company needs more space to take on extra staff.

Several people try to persuade the managing director and founder of the company, Sam King, to go for a modern warehouse building out of town. But he selects an old building in the dockland area.

Fitting in the computer system and desks proves challenging. This is made more difficult by Sam's insistence that parts of the main floor must be at different levels. The desks are arranged so that they are not all in straight lines.

Much of the original wooden flooring and old brick walls are left exposed. Fluorescent lighting is kept to a minimum, and large potted plants are placed amongst the desks.

Sam is criticised by many of his managers because a move to a brand new building would have been cheaper. However, the critics soon revise their views. The extra money spent is soon recouped, because the company's running costs are now much lower. The problems at their old premises, *ie* high staff turnover and too much sick leave, have disappeared.

Glossary

Aerobics. Continuous exercise, *eg* a brisk walk, which supplies oxygen to the muscles. The best form of exercise – replaces fatty muscle with lean muscle.

Astral influences. Influences which originate from outside the earth's atmosphere. The most important astral influence is sunlight.

Astrological calendar. The year divided into twelve equal periods – each one named after a star constellation in the zodiac belt. The time of year is marked by the position of the sun against these constellations.

Autonomic. The way in which the nervous system works. Meaning automatic, or with no apparent conscious intervention.

Balance point. Used to represent the point when you match your physical and emotional needs to what the environment has to offer. The point at which you are not being subjected to any excesses or deficiencies. The point you need to get to for physical and emotional well-being.

Bio-type. A shortened version of metabolic type or bio-chemical type. A classification – left or right bias – which describes how well your body processes food to extract energy, and material for building and maintenance.

Birth sign. The period in the astrological calendar, during which you were born. For example, Gemini – 21 May to 20 June. There are personality tendencies associated with each birth sign. The variation in personality is probably due to the effects of ultraviolet light levels on the unborn child. The personality tendencies can be used as part of a person's personal profile. Birth signs are also known as sun signs or zodiac signs.

Calorie controlled diet. Matching your energy requirements to the energy supplied by your food. In theory by reducing energy supplied, you should lose weight. But this does not take into account how well you deal with the different food types.

Caveman diet. An estimate of what our bodies were designed to consume: fat 18 per cent, protein 17 per cent, carbohydrate 65 per cent.

Celestial sphere. The imaginary inverted hemisphere over our heads, on which the stars appear to be fixed.

Central nervous system. The link between the brain and the muscles, using electrical impulses, which controls our movements.

Deficiency. A shortage of an item essential for well-being, for example the mineral selenium.

Endocrine nervous system. The nervous system which controls digestion. Works by glands releasing hormones into the blood stream. Linked to the left and right brain through the pituitary gland.

Excess. Something that is not an essential for well-being, and likely to do you harm, for example nicotine from cigarettes.

Exhaustion stage. Part of the unbalance and recovery cycle. The stage at which your body gives up the fight against an excess or a deficiency, and you notice something is wrong.

Far ultraviolet (UV-C). That part of ultraviolet radiation which does not reach the earth's surface. It is filtered out by the ozone in the upper atmosphere, and is fatal to life on earth.

Feng shui. The ancient Chinese art of ensuring you live in harmony with the forces of nature, through the correct arrangement of your living and working environment.

Food combining. The theory behind the **Hay diet**. This suggests that certain combinations of foods should be avoided to maximise efficiency of digestion process.

Free radical. An oxide within the body with nowhere to go. An excess of these can cause you harm, and is often the result of breathing in polluted air.

High architecture. Building design inspired by astral influences, for example cathedrals.

Hypersensitive stage. Part of the unbalance and recovery cycle. The stage after you have eliminated the excess or deficiency. Although you are back to well-being, you will now be much more sensitive to the item that caused the problem.

Hypothalamus. Located at the bottom of the brain, it tells the pituitary gland which hormones to release.

Left brain. The side that controls analytical thinking. It tends to dominate the right thinking side. The left side also looks after building, maintenance, and reproduction.

Metabolic typing. Devised by a Dr Kelley in America. Basic classification is according to a left or right bias of the nervous system. Dr Kelley's ideas go well beyond these classifications, at which point the theory becomes confusing. But the two basic classifications are helpful, as they give a good indication of foods with which you may have problems.

Minerals. Trace elements in food, *eg* zinc, which are essential for body building and maintenance.

Near ultraviolet. Present at the earth's surface. It is not visible, but is received by the eyes to inform the body of the day and night cycle. Also responsible for the production of vitamin D by its action on the skin.

Nervous system bias. A simple way of describing the two main metabolic type classifications: either left or right, or somewhere in between. Mainly used as an indicator of physical needs, but some emotional tendencies can also be deduced.

Oxidation. The process by which food is consumed or digested. The equivalent of fuel being burned in an engine.

Parasympathetic. The technical term for the nervous system controlled by the right side of the brain.

Pineal. Sometimes called the third eye. A gland inside the head which responds to ultraviolet levels through the eyes.

Pituitary. The gland which connects the brain, via the hypothalamus, to the nervous system.

RDA. Stands for recommended daily allowance. A useful guide for people taking vitamin and mineral supplements.

Right brain. The creative part of the thinking brain, but dominated by the left side. The right brain is also responsible for the nervous system which controls digestion and fighting infections.

Seasonally affective disorder. Often abbreviated to SAD. This is a feeling of depression due to a lack of natural daylight – either because of the winter, or too much time under artificial light.

Sensory influences. Effect our body and mind through our senses. Vision is the strongest receiver. Negative sensory influences can set off the stress reaction, for example for people who live in run-down housing. Positive sensory influences hold off the stress reaction, and make people feel calm. Buildings and interiors can be designed to have positive sensory influence.

Sick building syndrome. Some offices environments cause an above average level of staff sickness. Root causes may be negative sensory influences resulting from bad interior design, or a lack of natural daylight.

Sympathetic. The technical name for the nervous system controlled by the left side of the brain.

Terrestrial influences. Influences that originate at or just above the earth's surface. Can be physical or sensory, for example air temperature and music.

Vernacular architecture. Inspired by terrestrial influences. Very much part of the local landscape and culture. For example, cottages.

Vitamin. Substance, usually in food, that is essential for well-being and life.

Zodiac/zodiac belt. The band of twelve star constellations across which the sun passes, taking twelve months to go from start to finish. The forms the basis of the astrological, or zodiac calendar.

Further Reading

ASTRONOMY AND ASTROLOGY

Stars and Planets – Collins Pocket Guide, Ian Ridpath and Wil Tirion (Harper Collins, 2nd edition, 1996).
Zodiac Types – Collins Gem (Harper Collins, 1993).
The Lure of the Heavens (A History of Astrology), Donald Papon (Samuel Weiser Inc., New York, pb edition, 1980).

NUTRITION AND METABOLISM

Medicine's Missing Link, Tom and Carole Valentine (Thorsons, 1987).
Body Clock, edited by Dr Martin Hughes (Weidenfield & Nicolson, 1989).
The Optimum Nutrition Bible, Patrick Holford (Judy Piatkus Publishers Ltd, pb edition, 1998).

DAYLIGHT AND HEALTH

Health and Light, John N Ott (Devin-Adair Company Inc., 1976, pb edition, Ariel Press).

ARCHITECTURE AND HEALTH

Places of the Soul, Christopher Day (Aquarian Press/Thorsons, 1990).
Simply Feng Shui, Wendy Hobson (W Foulsham & Co Ltd, 1998).

CREATIVE THINKING AND THE BRAIN

The Healing Brain, Robert Ornstein and David Sobel (Macmillan, 1988).

Drawing on the Right Side of the Brain, Betty Edwards (Harper Collins, 1982).

STRESS MANAGEMENT

Controlling Anxiety, William Stewart (How To Books, 1998).
Thriving on Stress, Jan Sutton (How To Books, 1998).

FOOD AND DIET

Food Combining for Health, Doris Grant and Jean Joice (Thorsons, 1991).
The Hay Diet Made Easy, Jackie Habgood (Souvenir Press, 1997).
Secret Ingredients, Peter Cox and Peggy Brusseau (Bantam Books, 1997).

Useful Addresses

Holland and Barrett. Health food shops in most large towns and cities. They sell a wide range of vitamin and mineral supplements and publish a free magazine, available in their stores, with advice on nutrition and health.

International Tree Foundation, Sandy Lane, Crawley Down, West Sussex RH10 4HS. Tel: (01342) 712536. Fax: (01342) 718282. Works for the cause of trees, by planting and protecting at home and abroad. Offers free professional advice to members.

Daylight Studios, 89–91 Scrub Lane, London NW10 6QU. Tel: (0181) 964 1200. Fax: (0181) 964 1300. Suppliers of daylight bulbs and tubes.

Brett Martin Roofing Products Ltd, Higgins Lane, Burscough, Lancashire L40 8JB. Tel: (01704) 895345. Fax: (01704) 894229. Suppliers of polycarbonate roofing for conservatories.

Allergycare, 1 Church Square, Taunton, Somerset TA1 1SA. Tel: (01823) 325022. Fax: (01823) 325024. Food allergy tests on individuals, plus guidance on vitamin and mineral status. Testing is done at health food outlets and pharmacies.

Index

ACTH, 69, 74
adaption stage, 14, 82
addiction, 92, 93, 96
aerobics, 86
alcohol, 94
allergy, 91, 96
artificial light, 72
astral influences, 15, 118
astrologer, 28
astrology, 28, 35, 38
astrological calendar, 16, 29, 62
astronomy, 16
atmosphere, 15, 98
autonomic, 19

balance point, 11
bio chemical, 18
bio-type, 18, 52, 84, 89, 110
bio-typing, 20
birth date, 16
birth sign, 28
black light, 66
blood stream, 17
buildings, 61, 114

caffeine, 95
calorie, 85
calorie controlled diet, 85
carbohydrates, 87
carbon dioxide, 66, 85
cars, 87, 98
caveman diet, 87, 97
celestial sphere, 25

central nervous system, 17
chocolate, 95
chromium, 107
cigarettes, 93
coffee, 94
computers, 75
conservatory, 71
constellation, 15
contact lenses, 67
creative thinking, 18

daylight, 60, 70, 76, 114
daylight bulbs, 73, 74
deficiency, 12, 102
diets, 86, 88
digestion, 17, 86, 92, 96
digital, 18
drugs, 92, 115

electromagnetic radiation, 64, 76, 99
endocrine nervous system, 17, 19, 115
environment, 11, 15
excess, 12, 90
exercise, 86, 87
exhaustion stage, 14, 82
eyes, 66, 68, 78

far ultraviolet, 64
fat, 87, 89, 97
feng shui, 116
fibre, 87
fish, 89, 98

flotation tank, 116
fluorescent lighting, 73
food combining, 88
free radical, 98
full spectrum lighting, 73
functional buildings, 118

glass, 66, 71
glasses, 67
greenhouse effect, 66

Hay's diet, 88
high-rise flats, 115
high architecture, 118
hormones, 17
hypersensitive stage, 14
hypothalamus, 68

incandescent lighting, 73

kilocalories, 85

left brain, 18, 20

meat, 87, 89
menstrual cycle, 53
mentor, 107
metabolic typing, 18
metabolism, 56, 86, 89-90
minerals, 101, 106
mobile phones, 101
moon, 16
moonlight, 15

near ultraviolet, 64, 66, 84
negative sensory influence, 116
nervous system, 17, 68, 70, 93
nervous system bias, 20, 55
nicotine, 93
nitrogen, 84

northern hemisphere, 25, 31
nuts, 95

ophiuchus, 36
optic nerve, 68
overweight, 84
oxidation, 86
oxides, 98
oxygen, 84
ozone, 66, 98

parasympathetic, 19
personal action plan, 107
personality, 16, 38, 39, 57, 71
pineal, 69, 70
pituitary, 19, 69
planets, 16
pollution, 61, 98
polycarbonate, 71
positive sensory influence, 117
power lines, 101
pregnancy, 64, 107
protein, 88
psychometric test, 58

radiation, 64, 99
RDA, 104
relationships, 12, 92
right brain, 18, 19
risk, 90

salt, 96
seasonally affected disorder, 69
selenium, 98, 104
sensory influences, 15, 114, 117
sensory messages, 84
seven stars, 16
sick building syndrome, 74, 117
skin, 70, 78
smoking, 93

solarium, 73
southern hemisphere, 25, 31, 39
stars, 15, 25
star map, 16, 35
stress, 69, 74, 91, 115
sugar, 95
sun, 15, 26, 61, 64, 71
sunbathing, 77
sun sign, 38
supplements, 102
sympathetic, 20

terrestrial influences, 15, 118
third eye, 69
tobacco, 93
toxins, 100
trees, 67, 72
Tropic of cancer, 35

ultraviolet, 64, 67
unbalance, 13, 82, 88
UV-A, 66, 73
UV-B, 66, 73
UV-C, 64, 66, 98

vegetarian, 102
vernacular architecture, 118
vitamin, 60, 101, 103-105

wavelength, 64
windows, 66

yoga, 115, 116

zodiac, 16, 31
zodiac belt, 26, 27
zodiac calendar, 28, 62